Kawanabe
Kyosai's Drawings for Fun

Vol I

ISBN: 9798634032542

© 2020 Livingston Libraries

All images from the Metropolitan Museum.

Kawanabe Kyosai's Drawings for Fun Vol I and II are the same aspect ratio as the original. While the manufacturing, type of paper, and inks might be different, the essence of Kyosai's style and personality shine through no less powerfully.

Kawanabe Kyosai

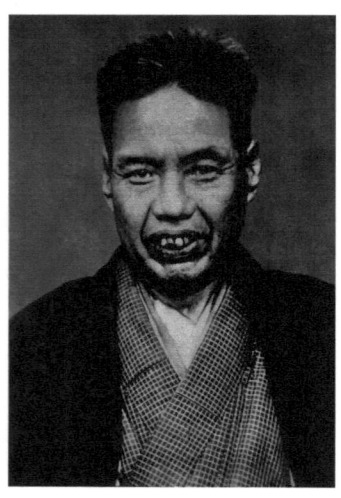

Kyosai - before 1889

Kawanabe Kyosai lived through Japan's transformmation from a feudal society to a modern state. Born 1831 in Koga in modern Ibaraki Prefecture, he trained in the Kano school of Japanese art. As a boy he worked for a short time with famed woodblock artist Utagawa Kuniyoshi.

For centuries, the Kano School was a heralded school in Japanese aesthetic design. During the 1867 revolution, Kyosai was known more as a caricaturist. He was arrested three times by the Tokugawa Shogunate, the feudal government he lived to see overthrown. He then went on to criticize the new constitutional monarchy headed by Emperor Meiji.

Kyosai succeeded renowned Japanese artist Hokusai - you may have seen his *Great Wave of Kanagawa* somewhere - as one of the great artists of Japanese history. His art evokes the traditional aesthetic, but betrays his unease with the world. His subjects are concerned with the changes brought by modern life, wildlife and nature.

The collection of Kyosai's birds, nature, and more are housed at the Metropolitan Museum in New York.

Drawing for Fun Vol. I and II

The Kano school of Japanese art was a major force in Japan until the Meiji Period. Although developed to decorate castles and screens, Kano flourished with many distinct periods depending on the personalities of their respective masters.

Kano Masanobu, the founder of the Kano school, was the first to paint scenes of zen buddhism and bodhisattvas on gold screens. It would only have been available to a select few aristocrats. Kawanabe Kyosai's art, by contrast, was widely printed and distributed using woodblock prints. His work was often developed for wider public consumption.

Drawing for fun is a reflection of that which we choose to mirror in our lives. Kyosai found joy in many scenes of nature. *Drawings for Fun* was a two-part art book created by Kyosai. As you enjoy his work, reflect upon that which you might draw for fun.

Capture your unique perspective on paper. Modern Japanese designer Marie Kondo poses the big question: "What sparks your joy?"

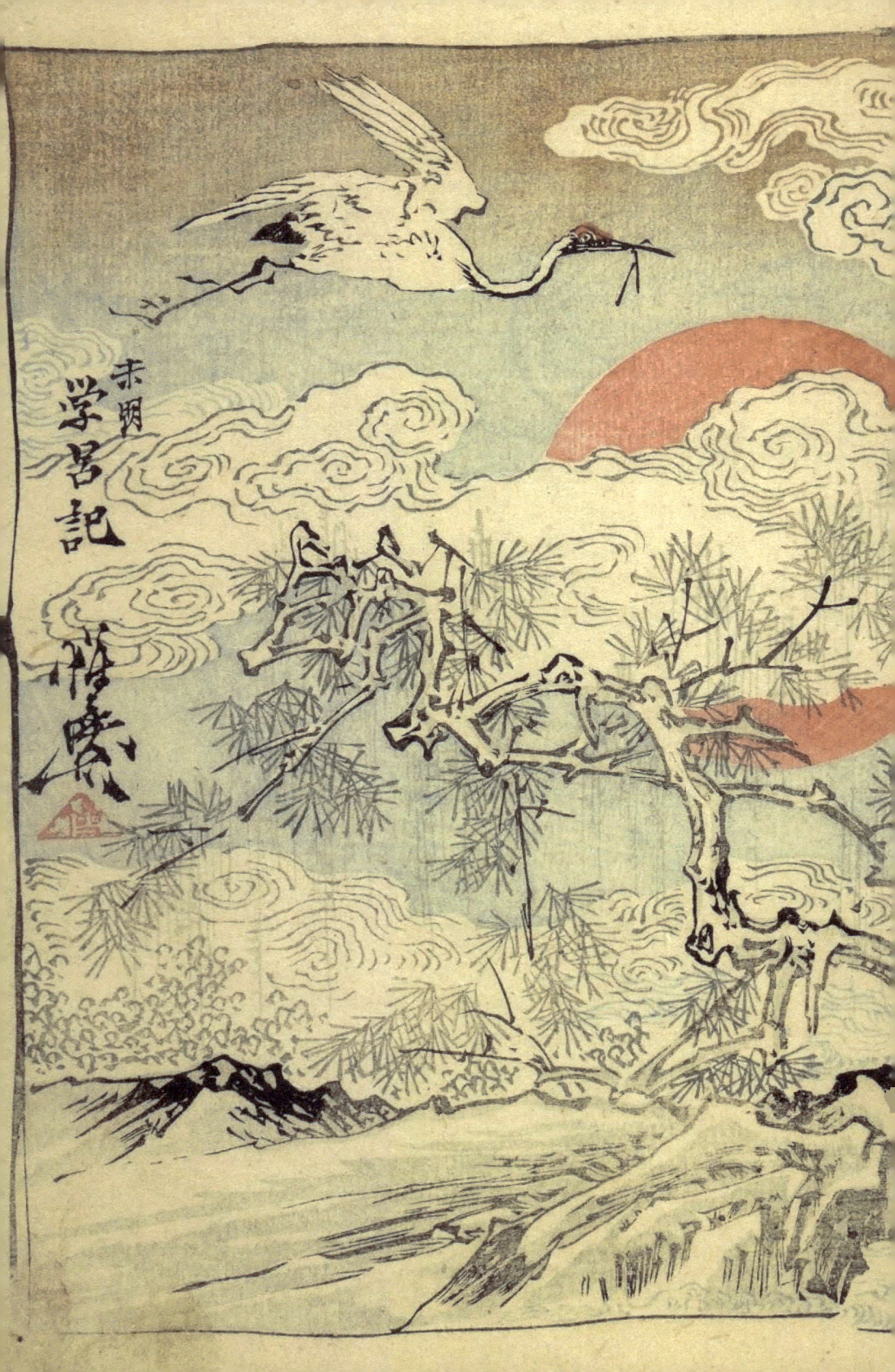

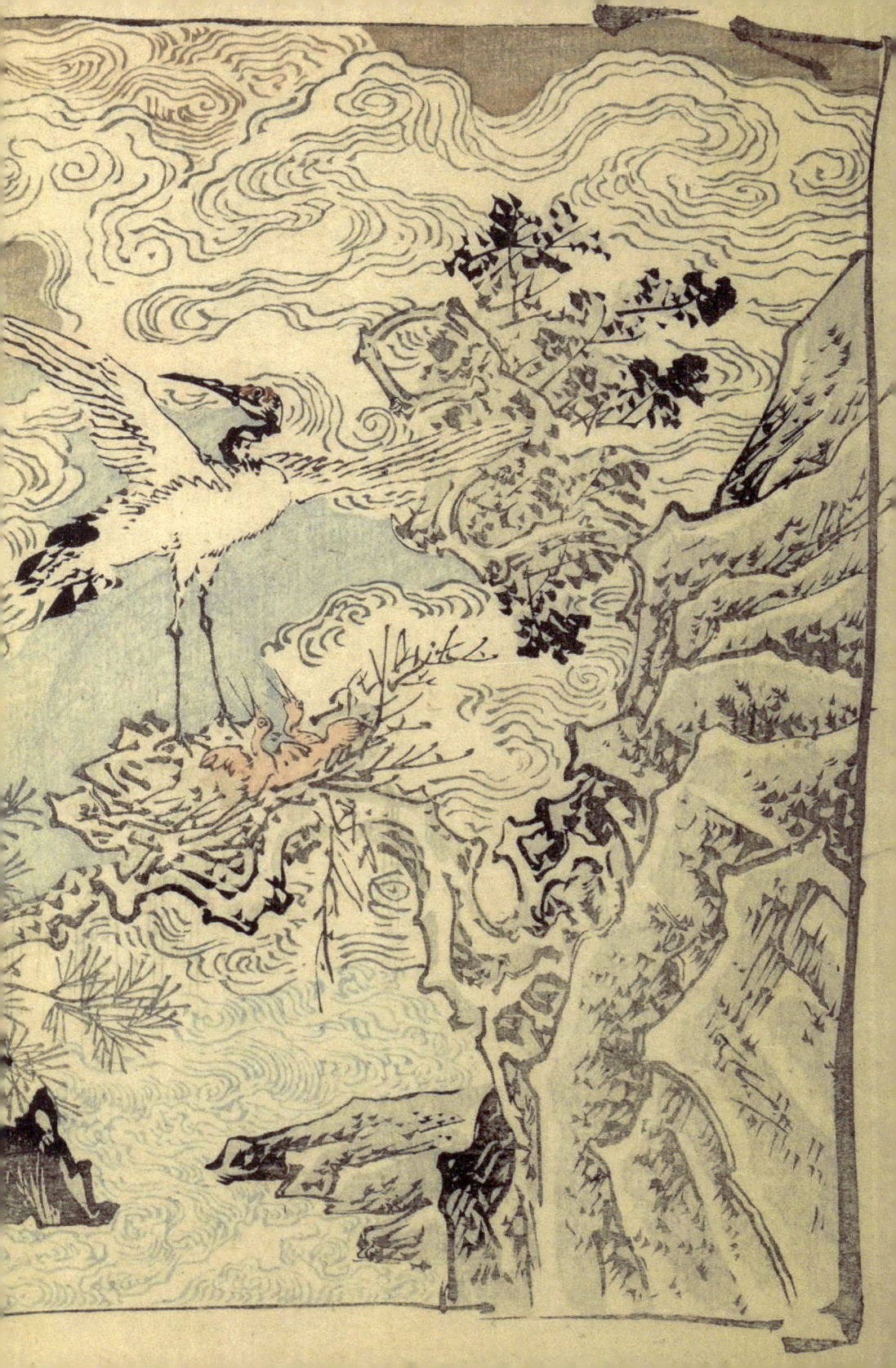

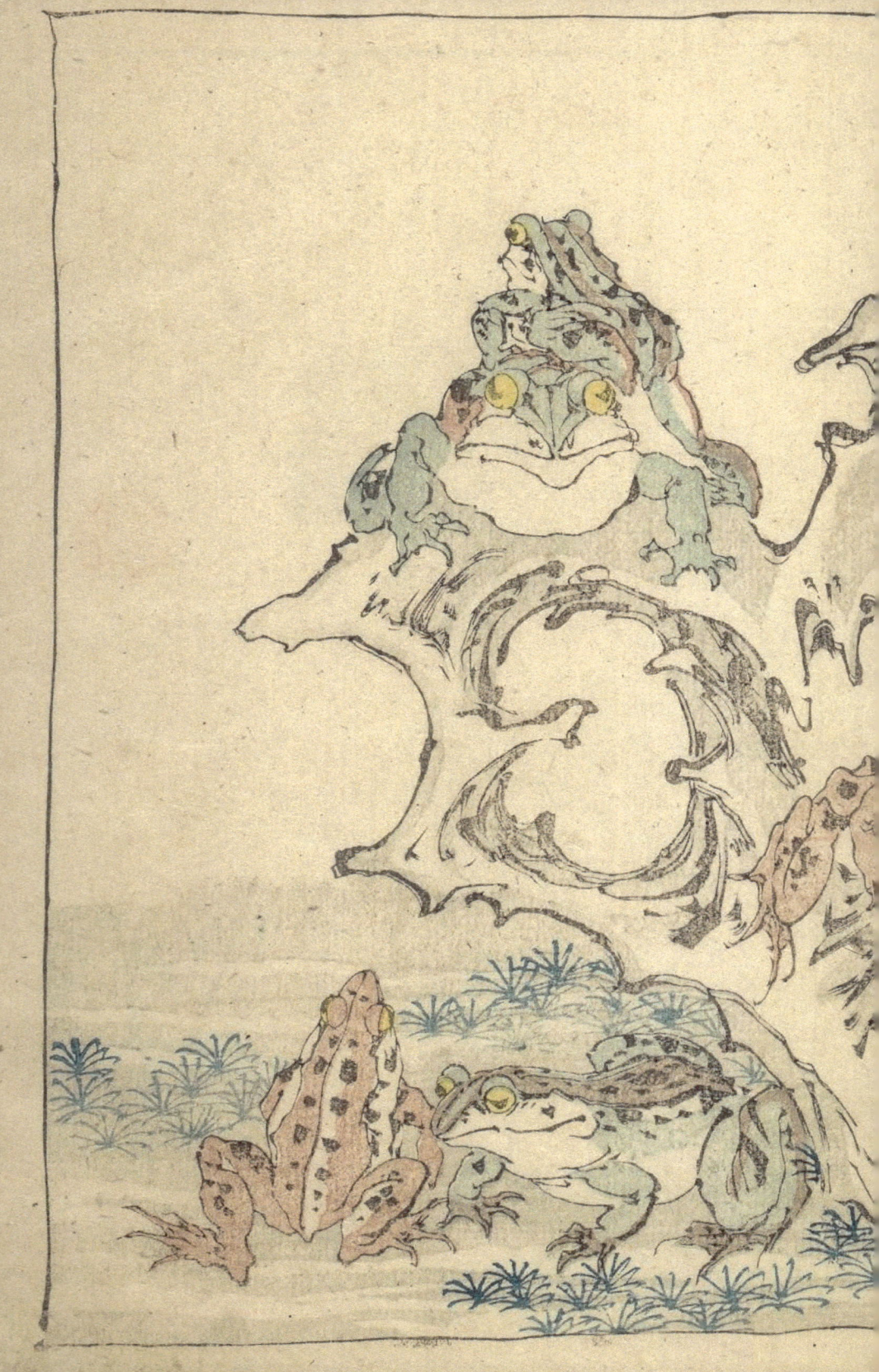

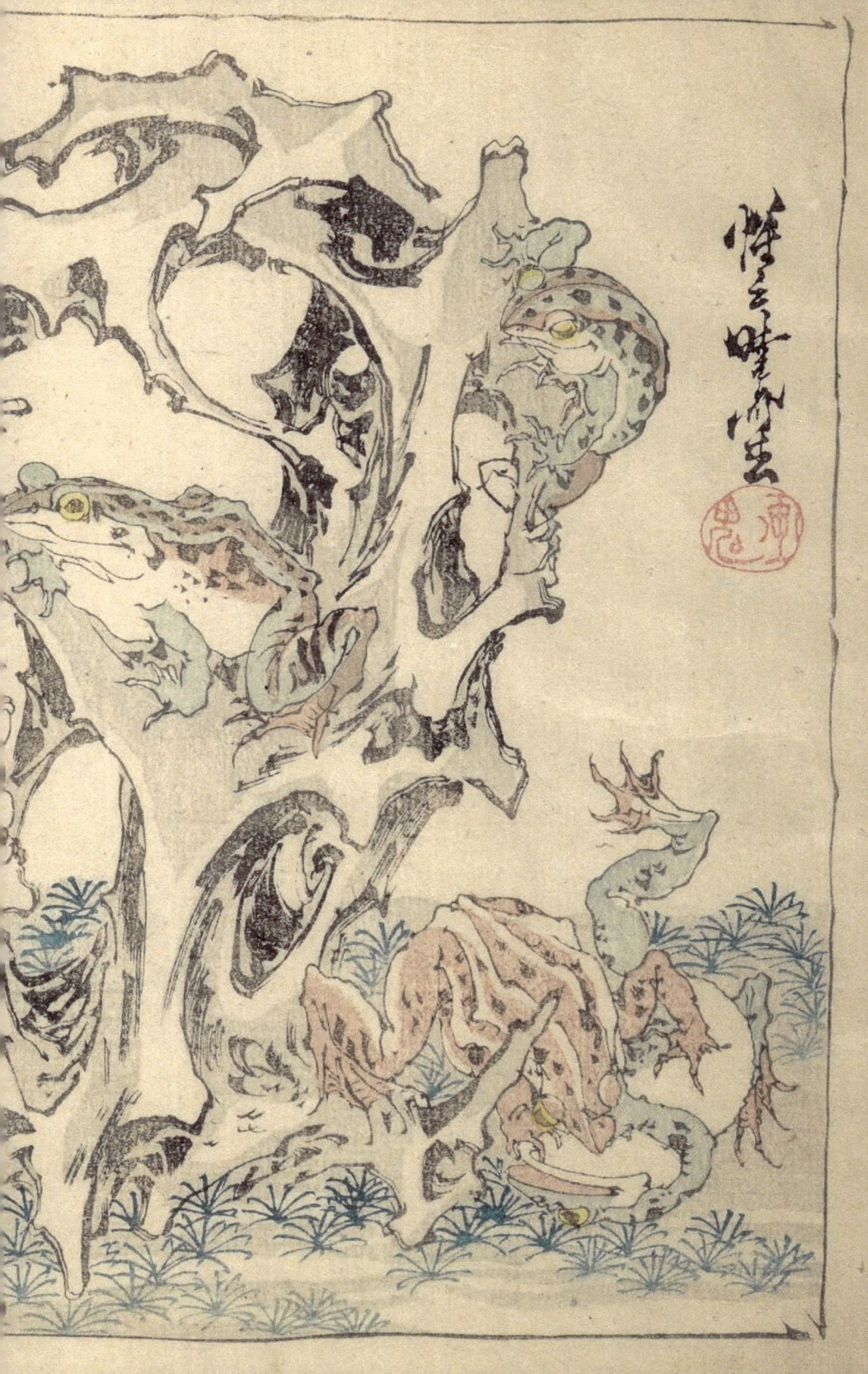

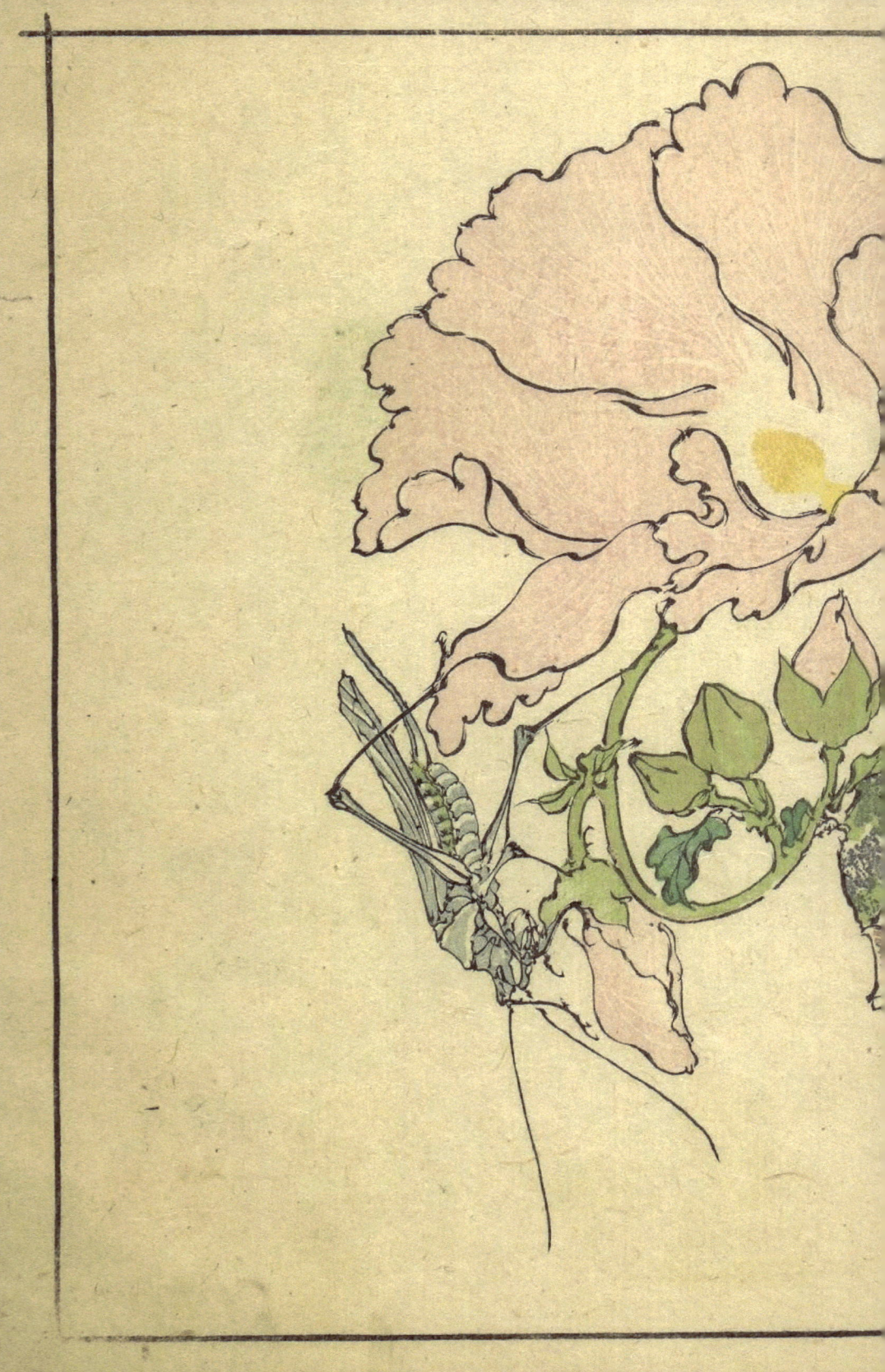

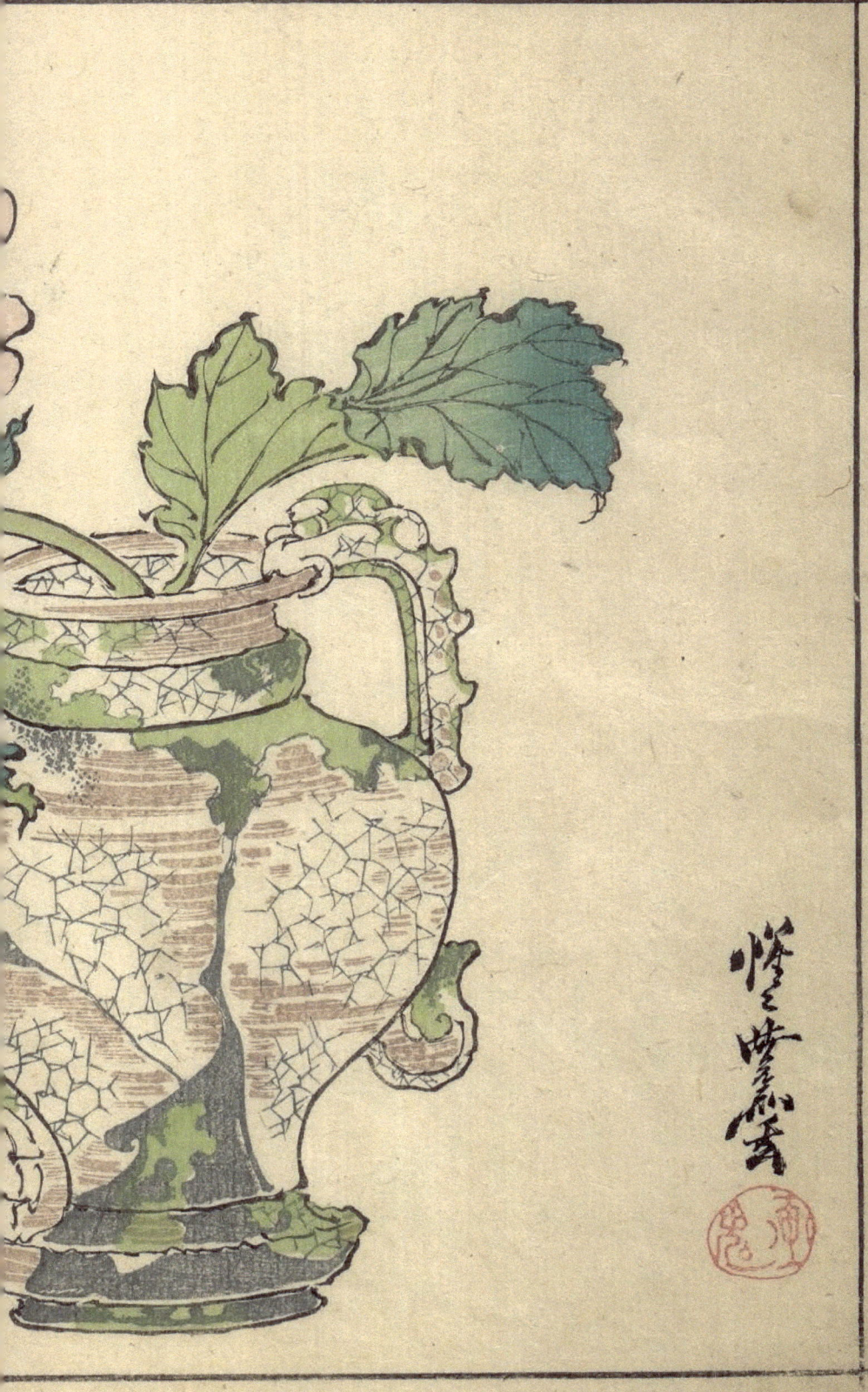

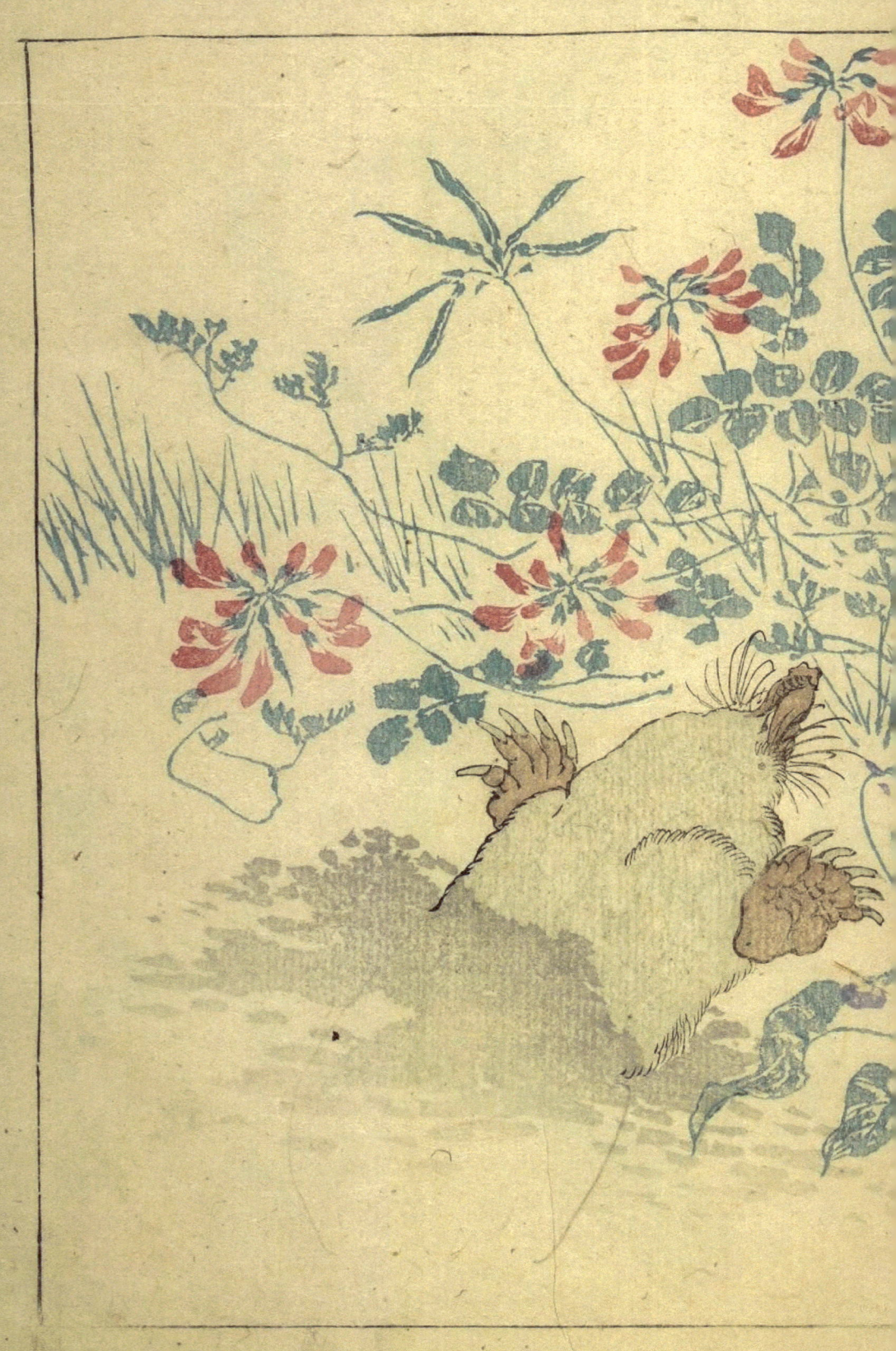

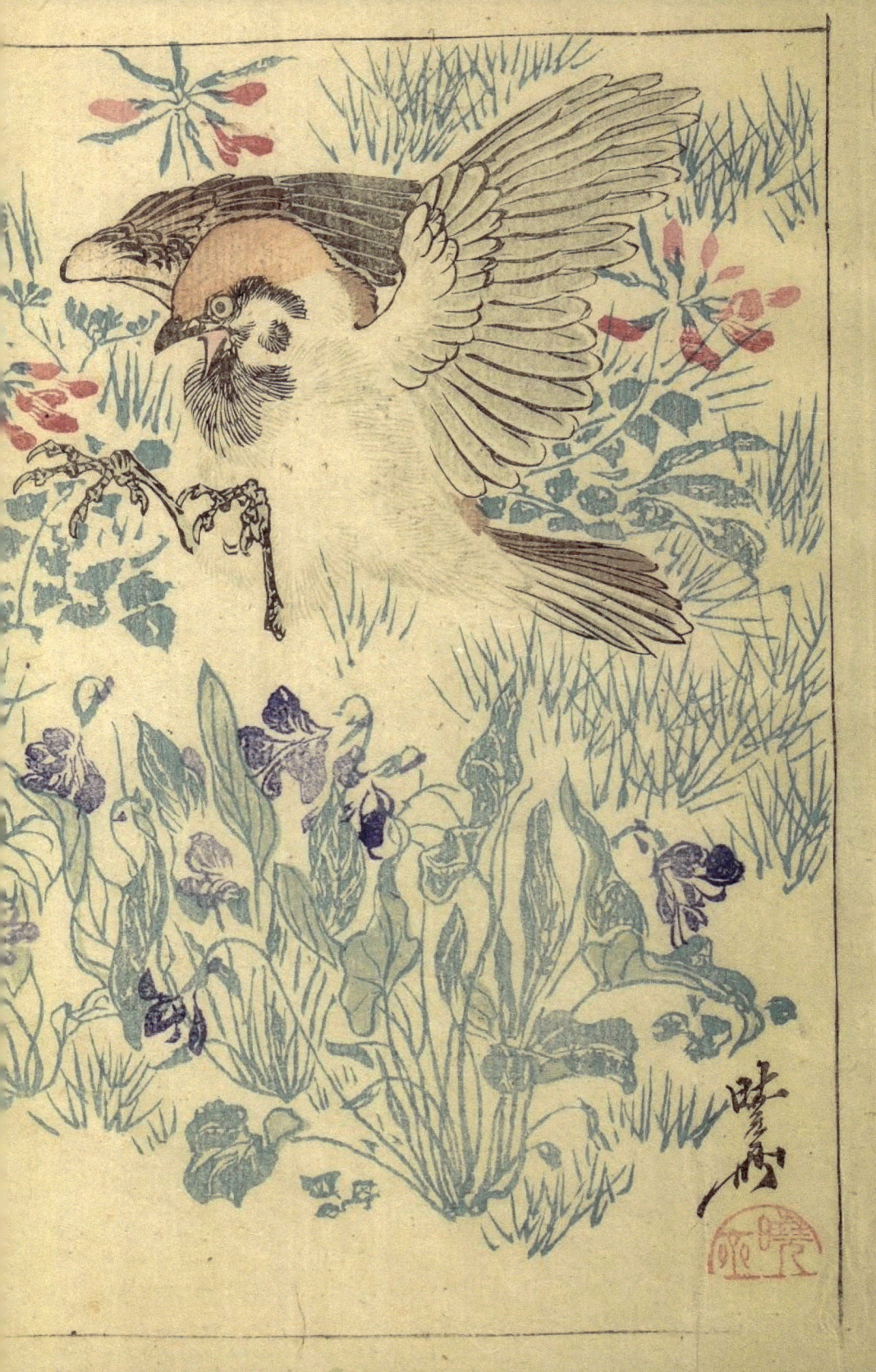

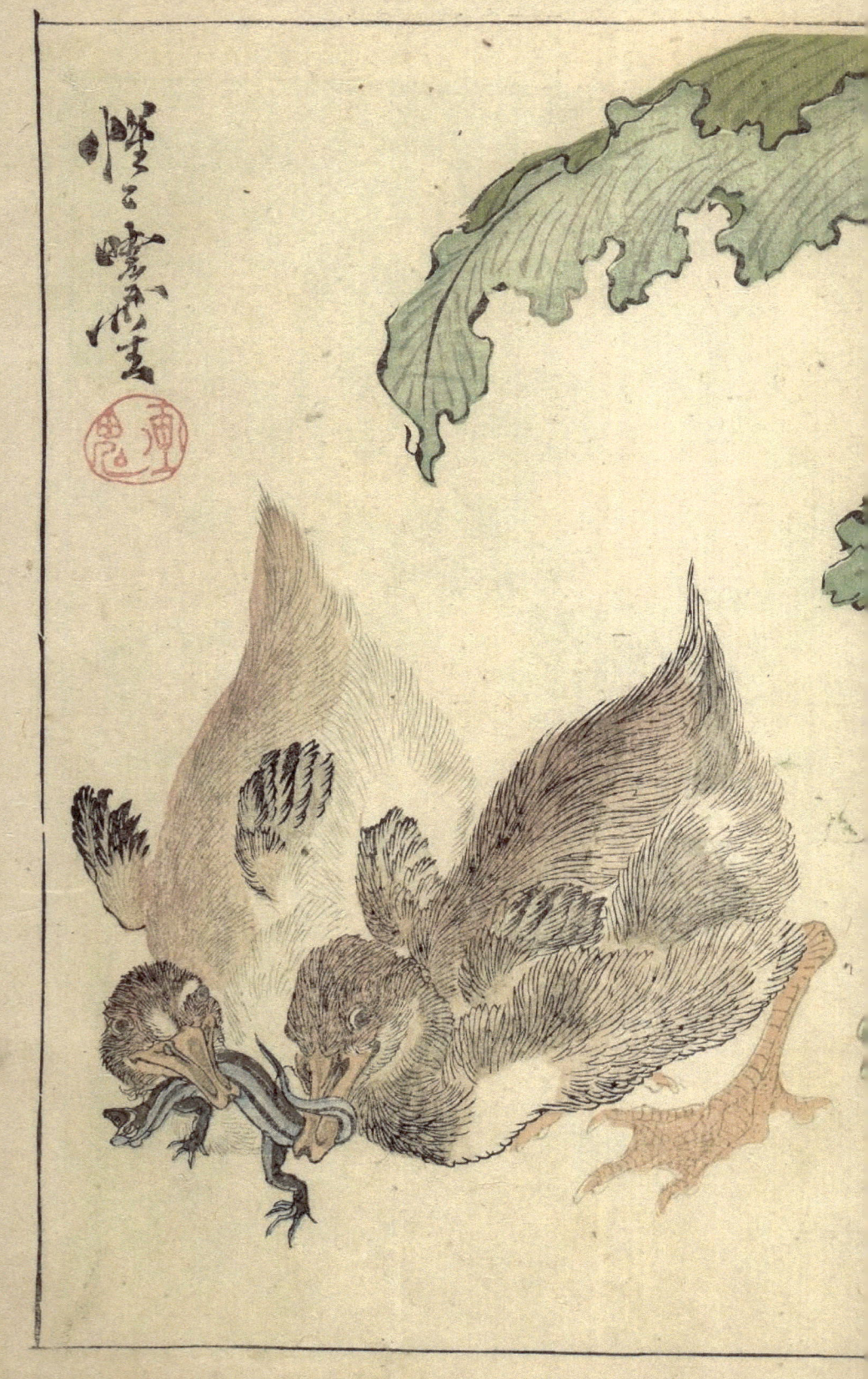

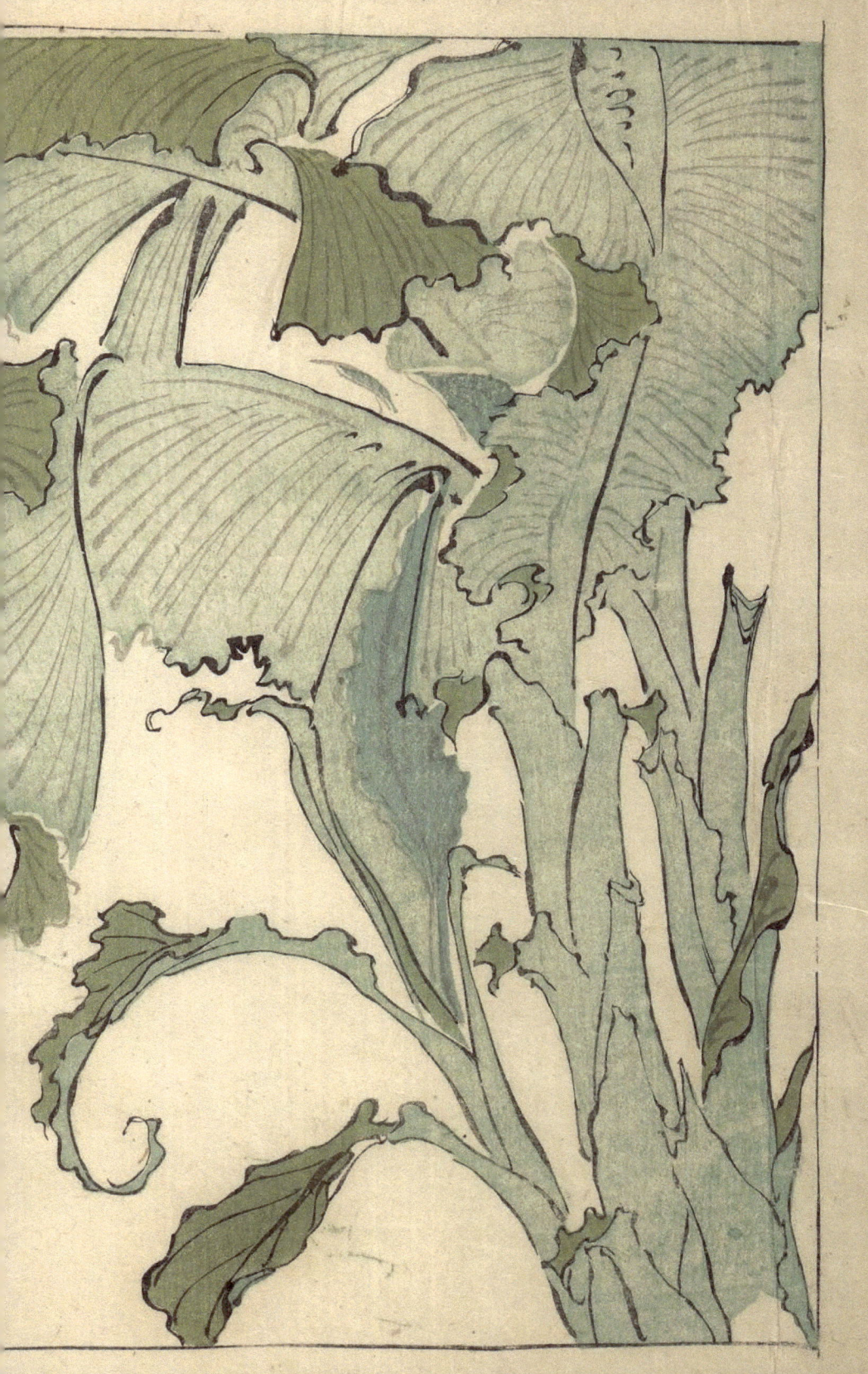

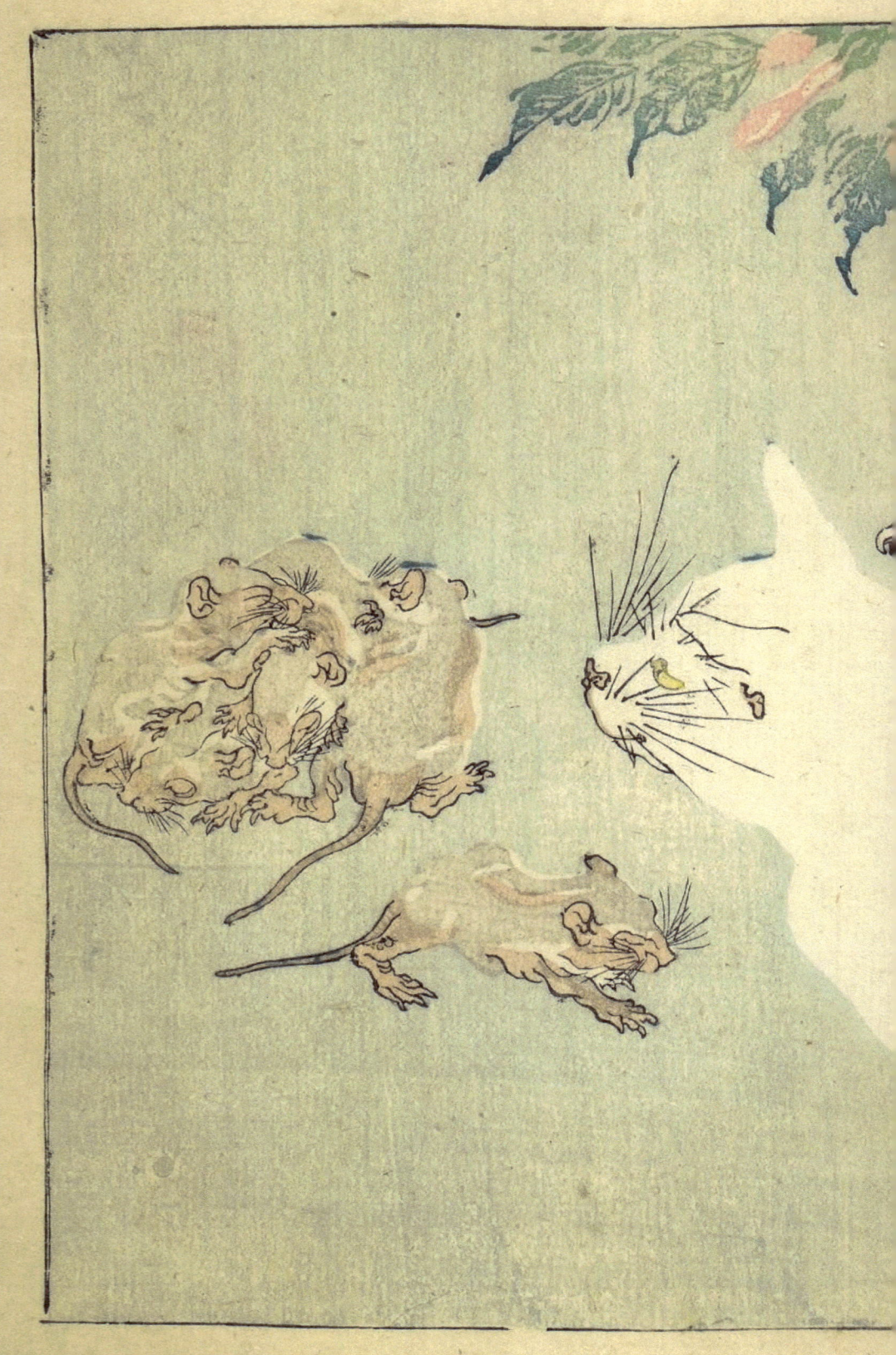

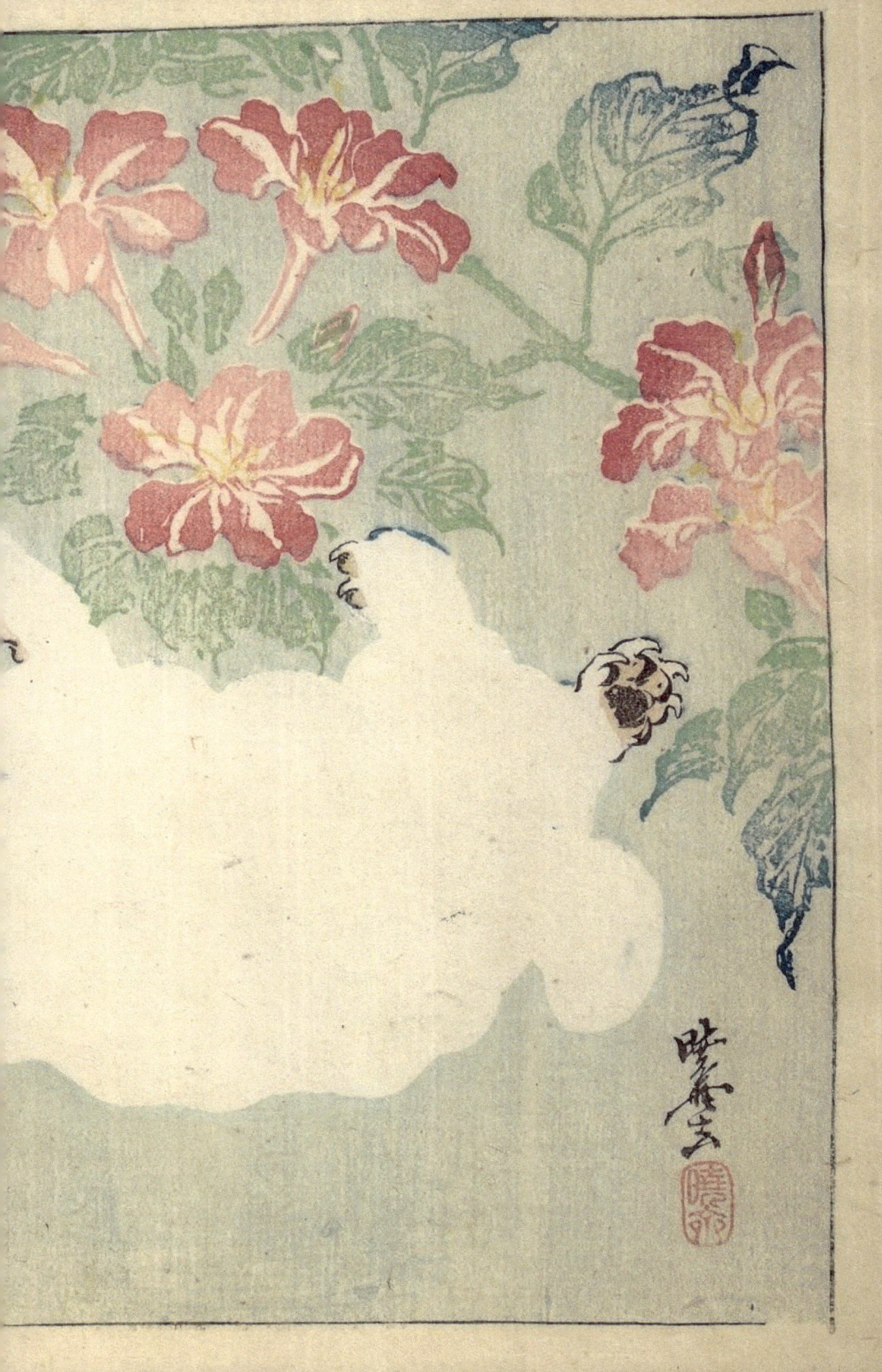

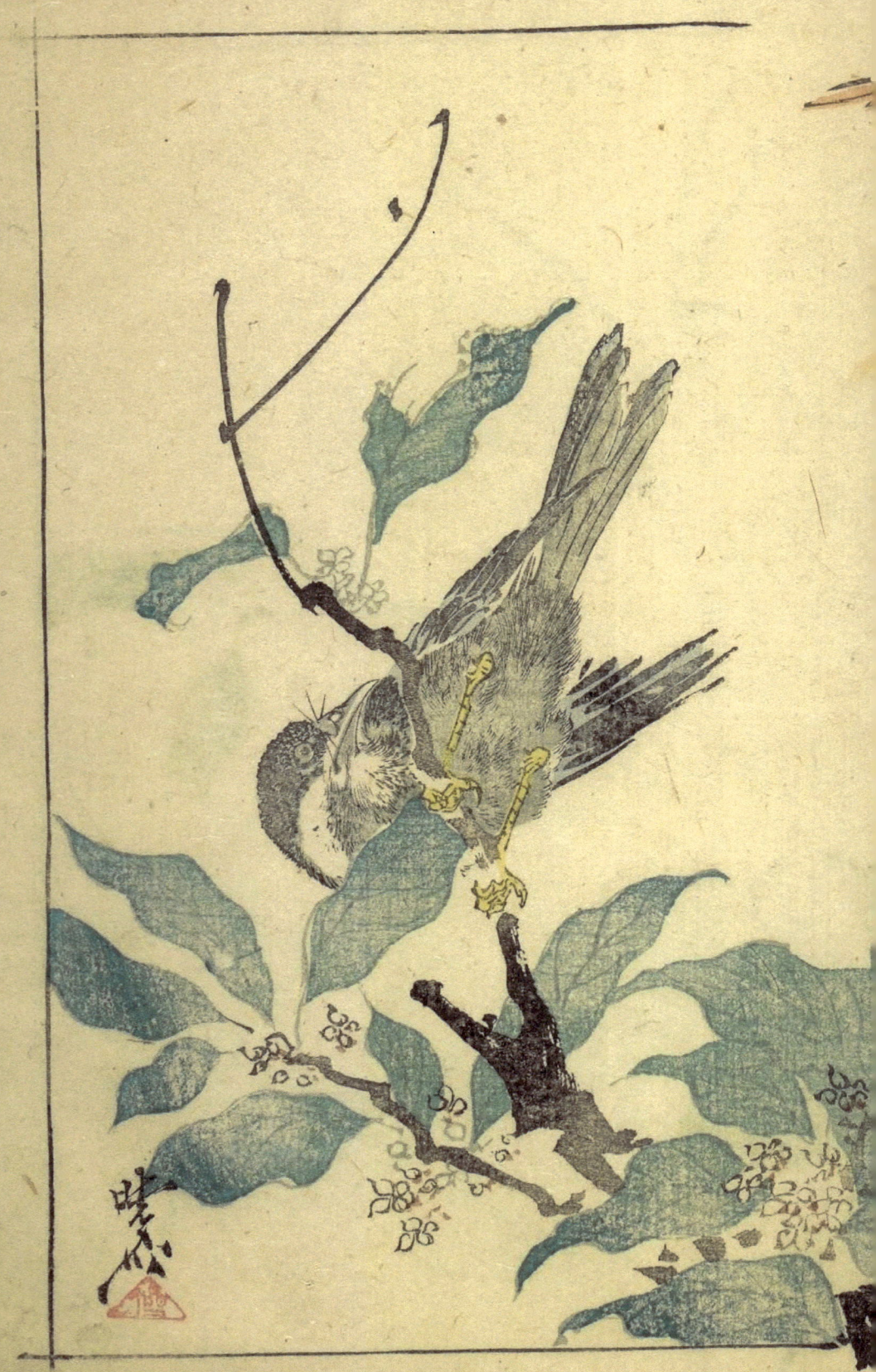

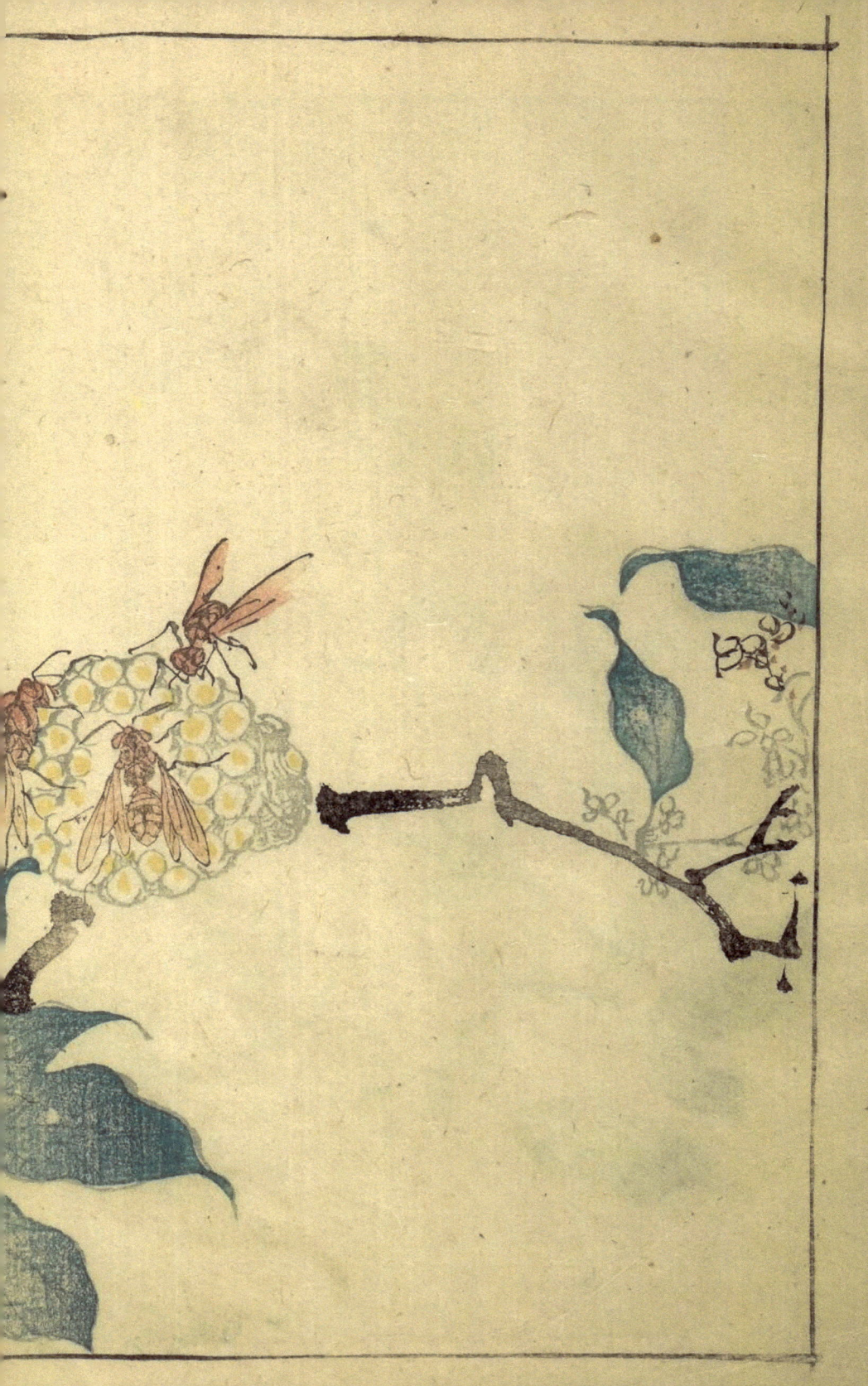

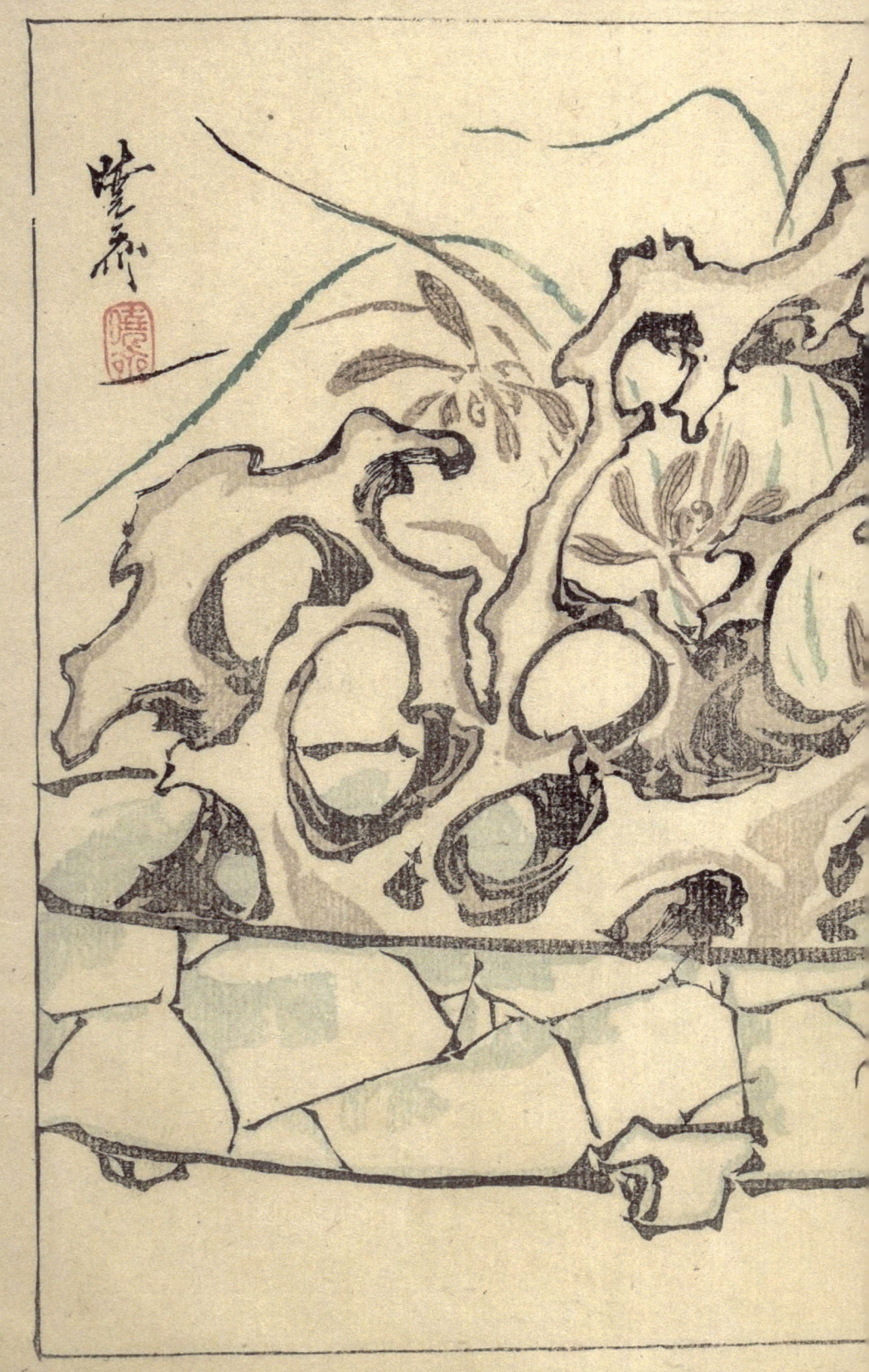

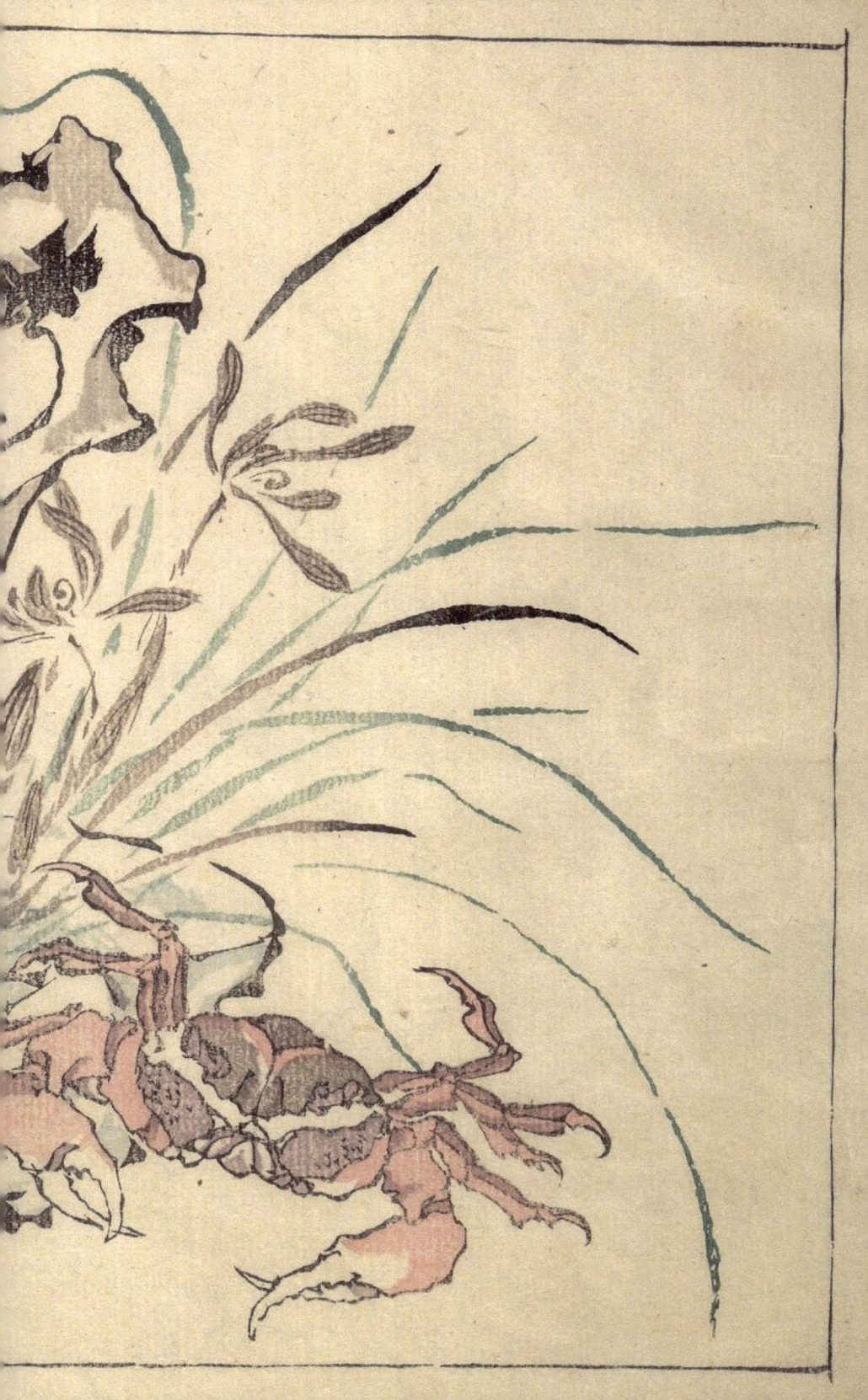

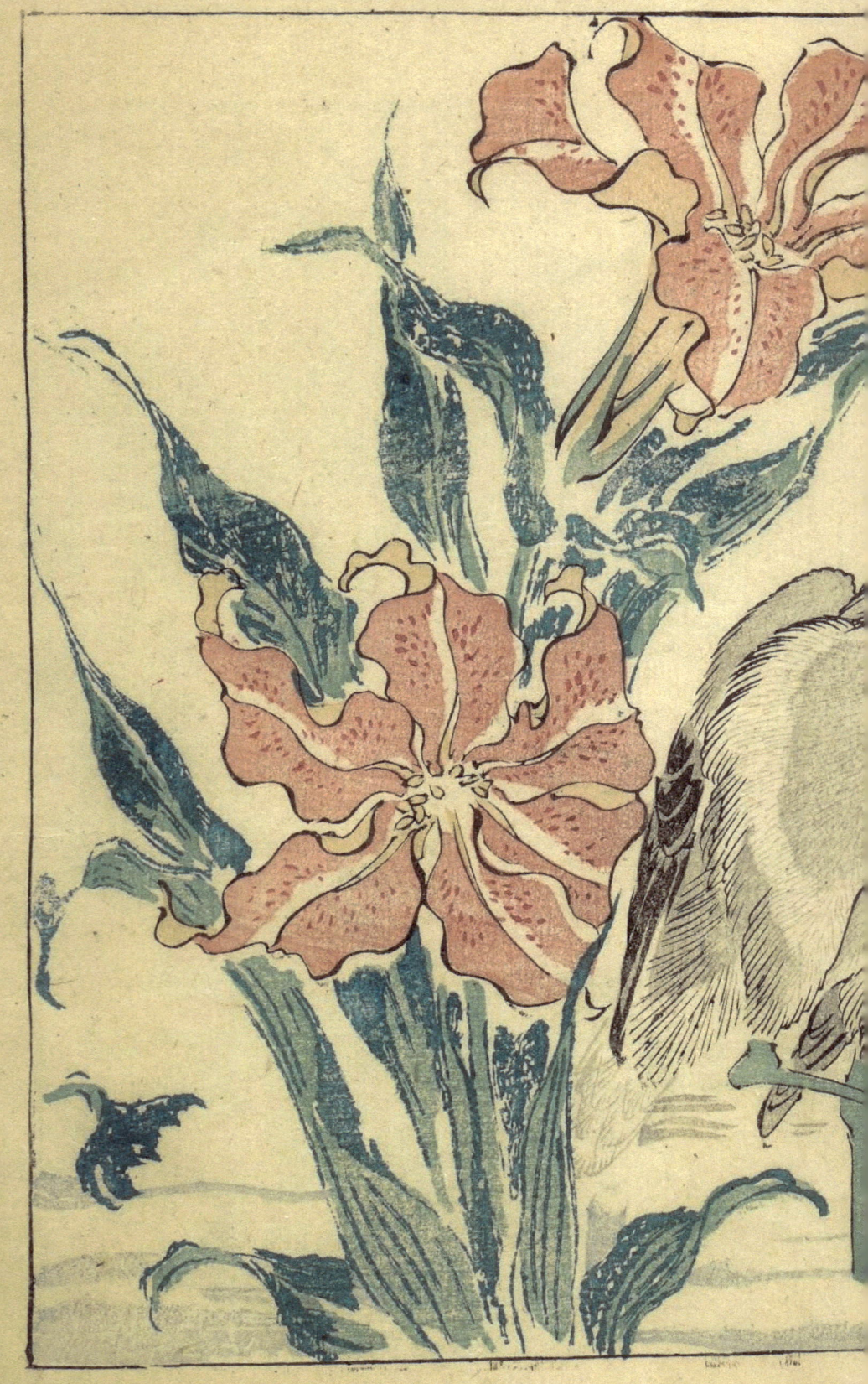

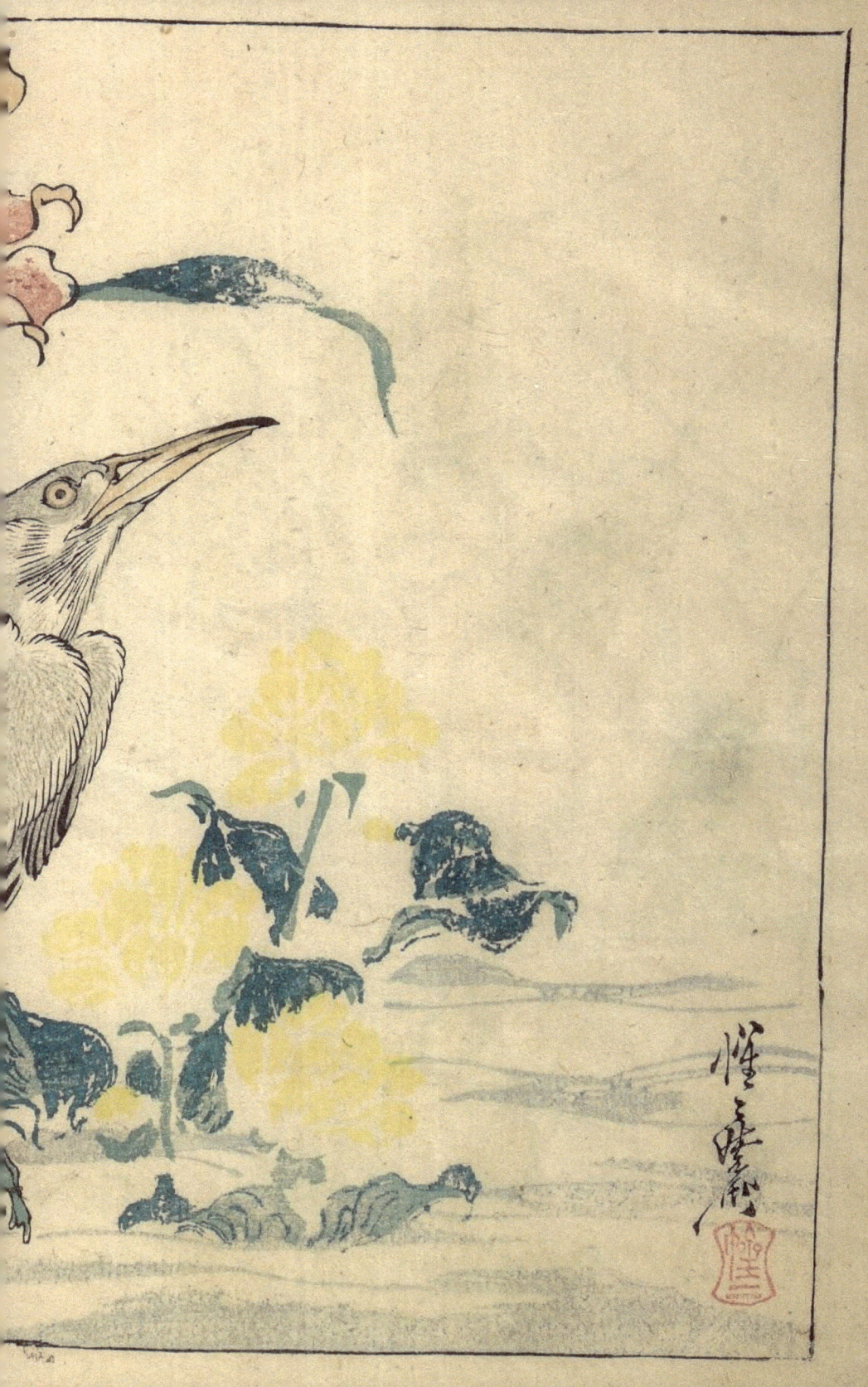

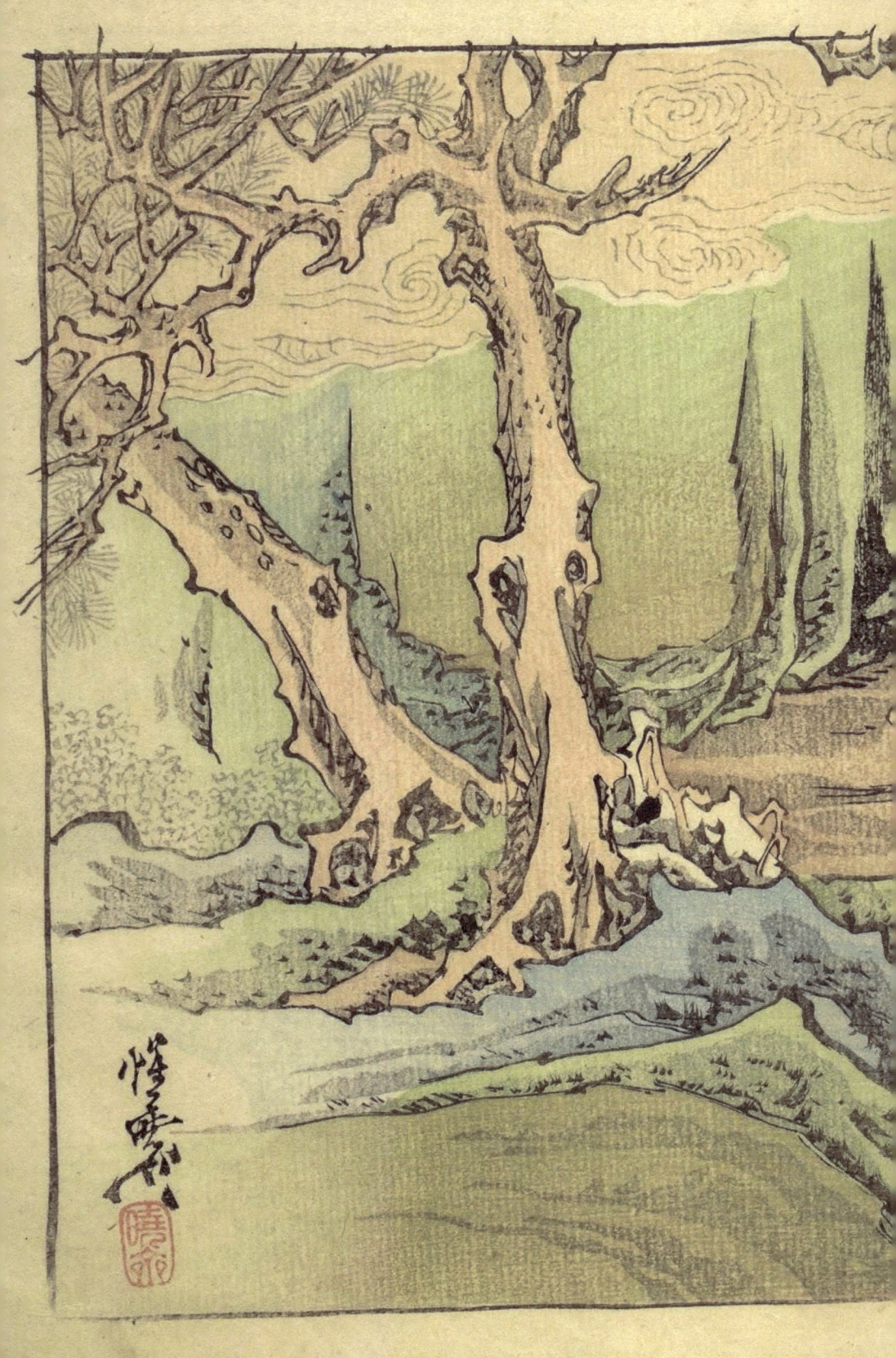

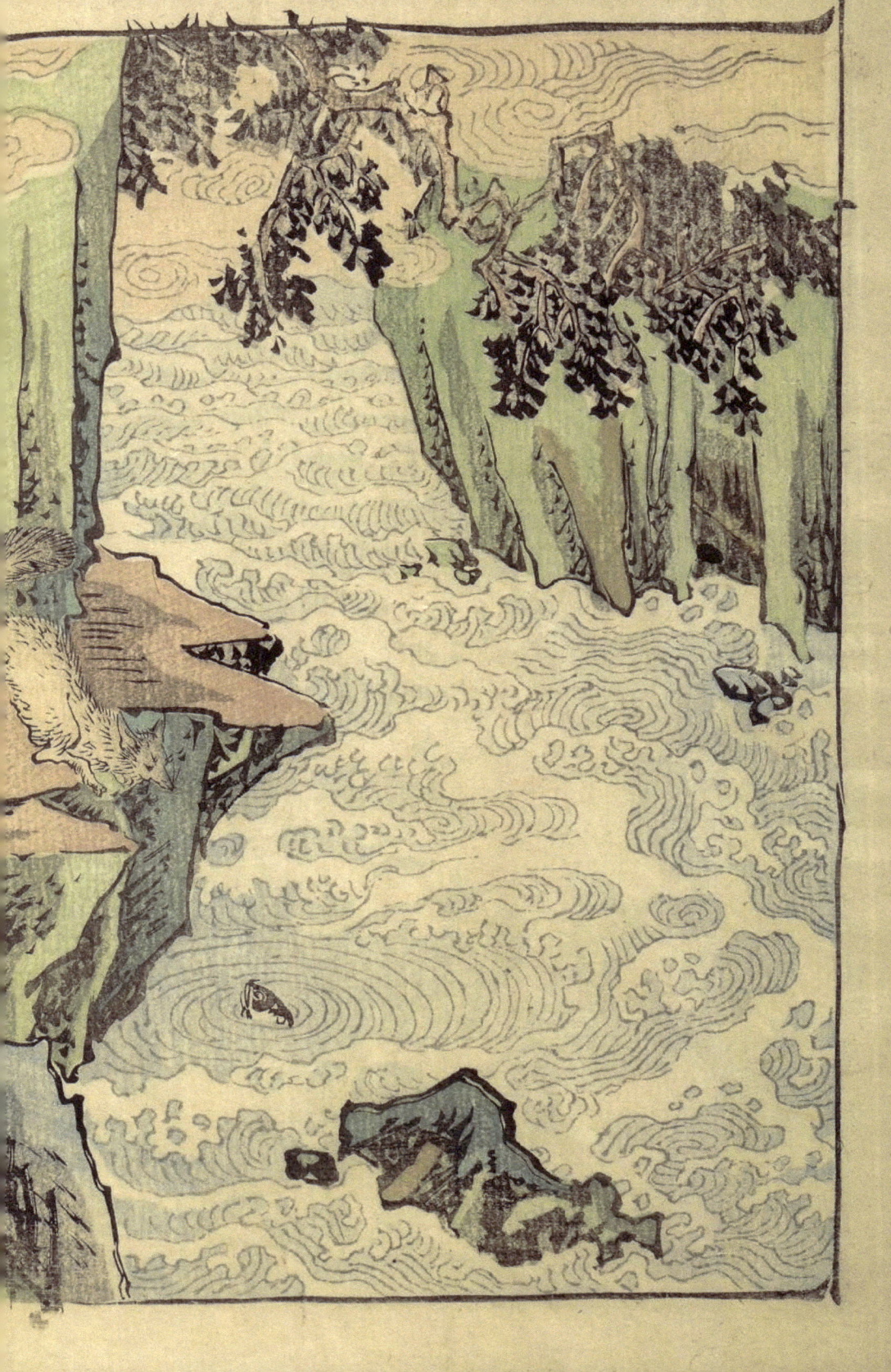

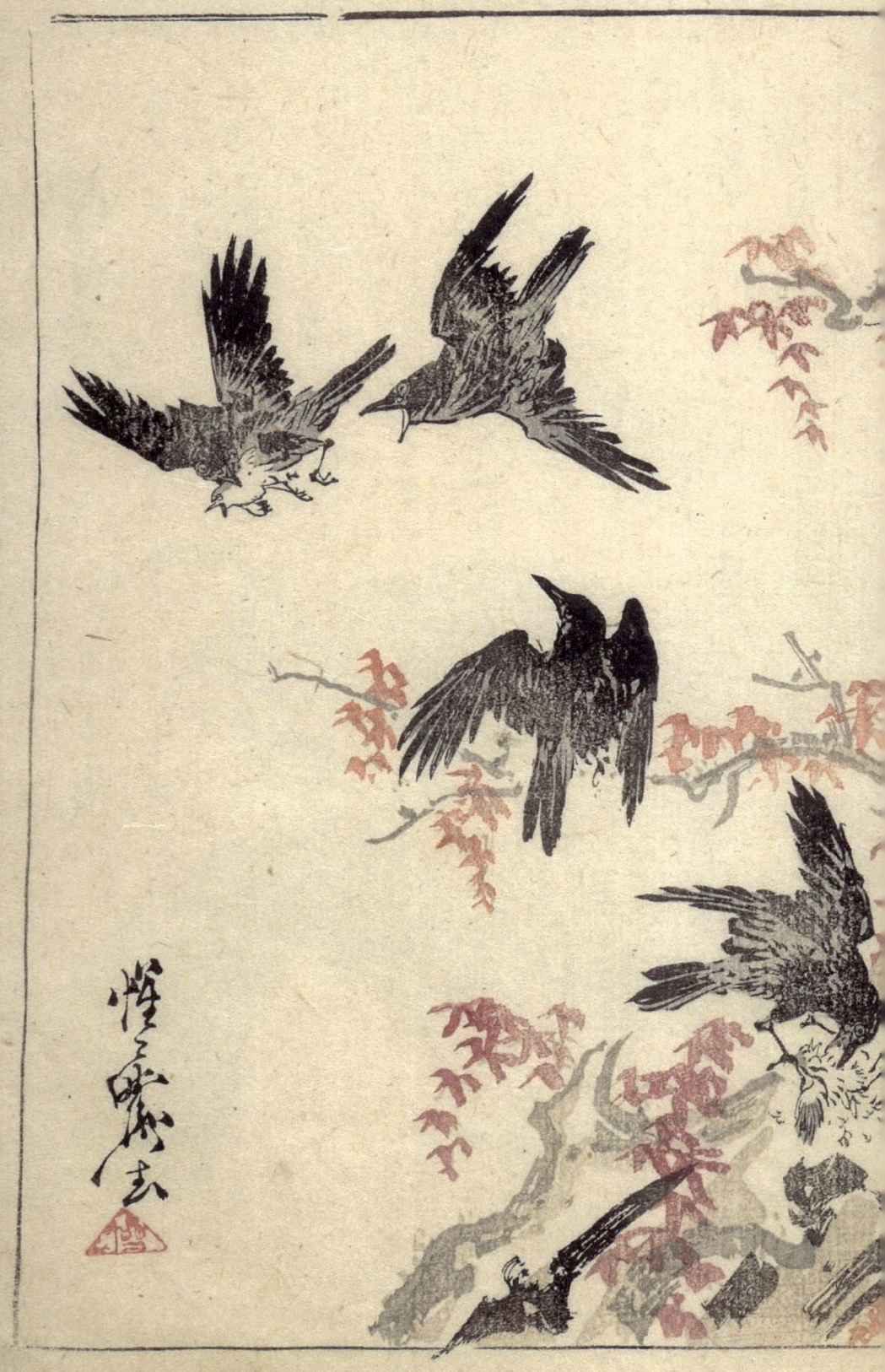

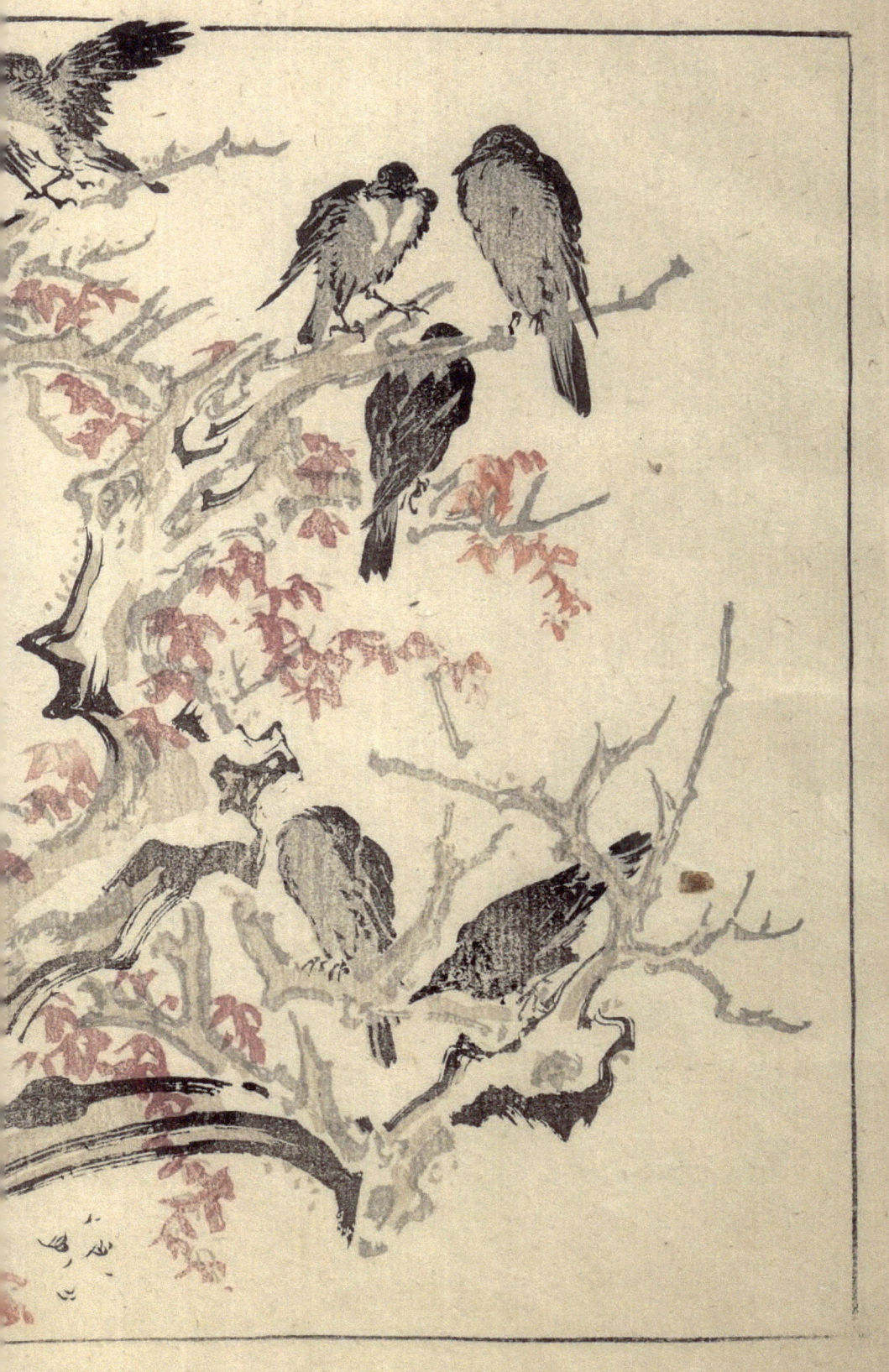

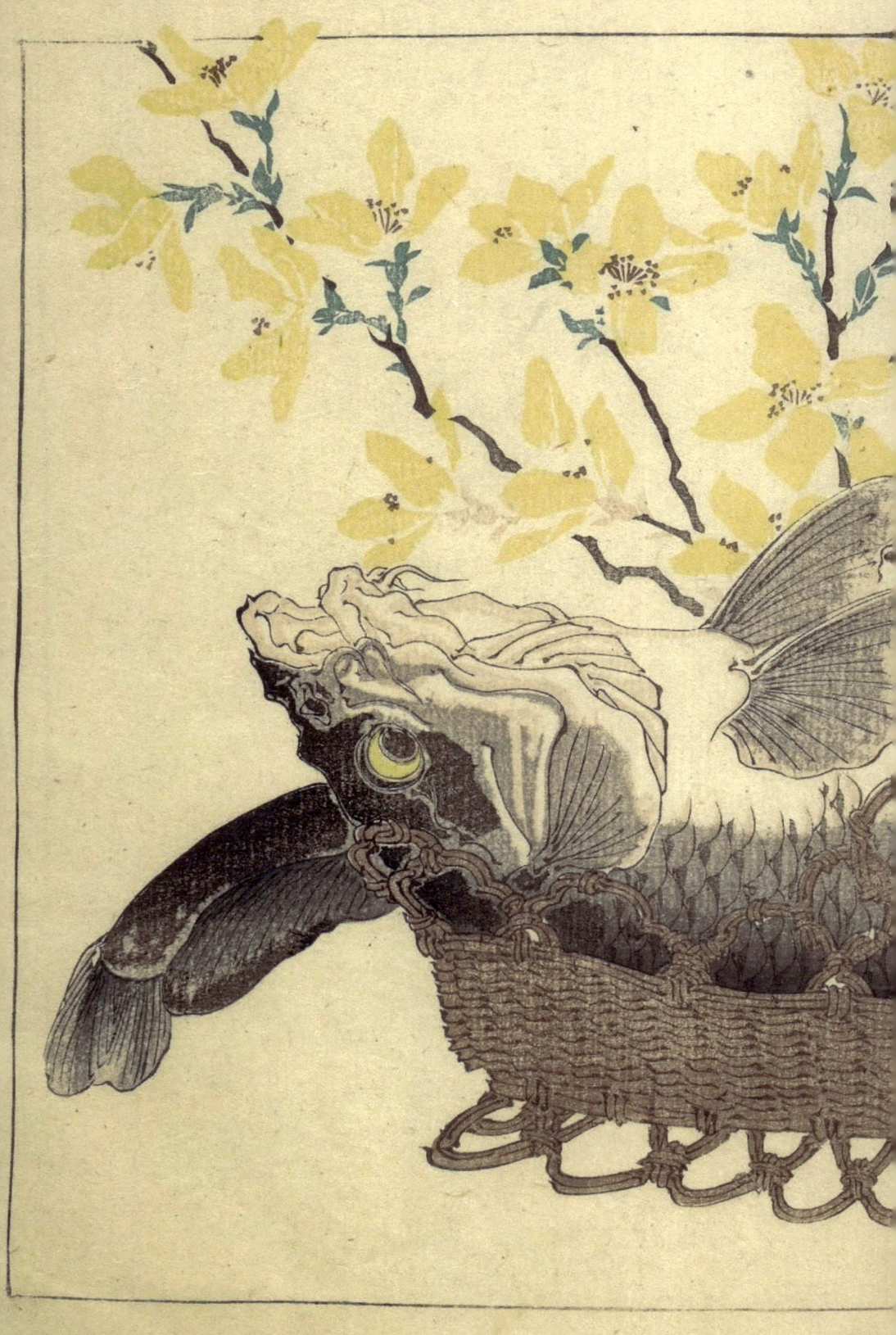

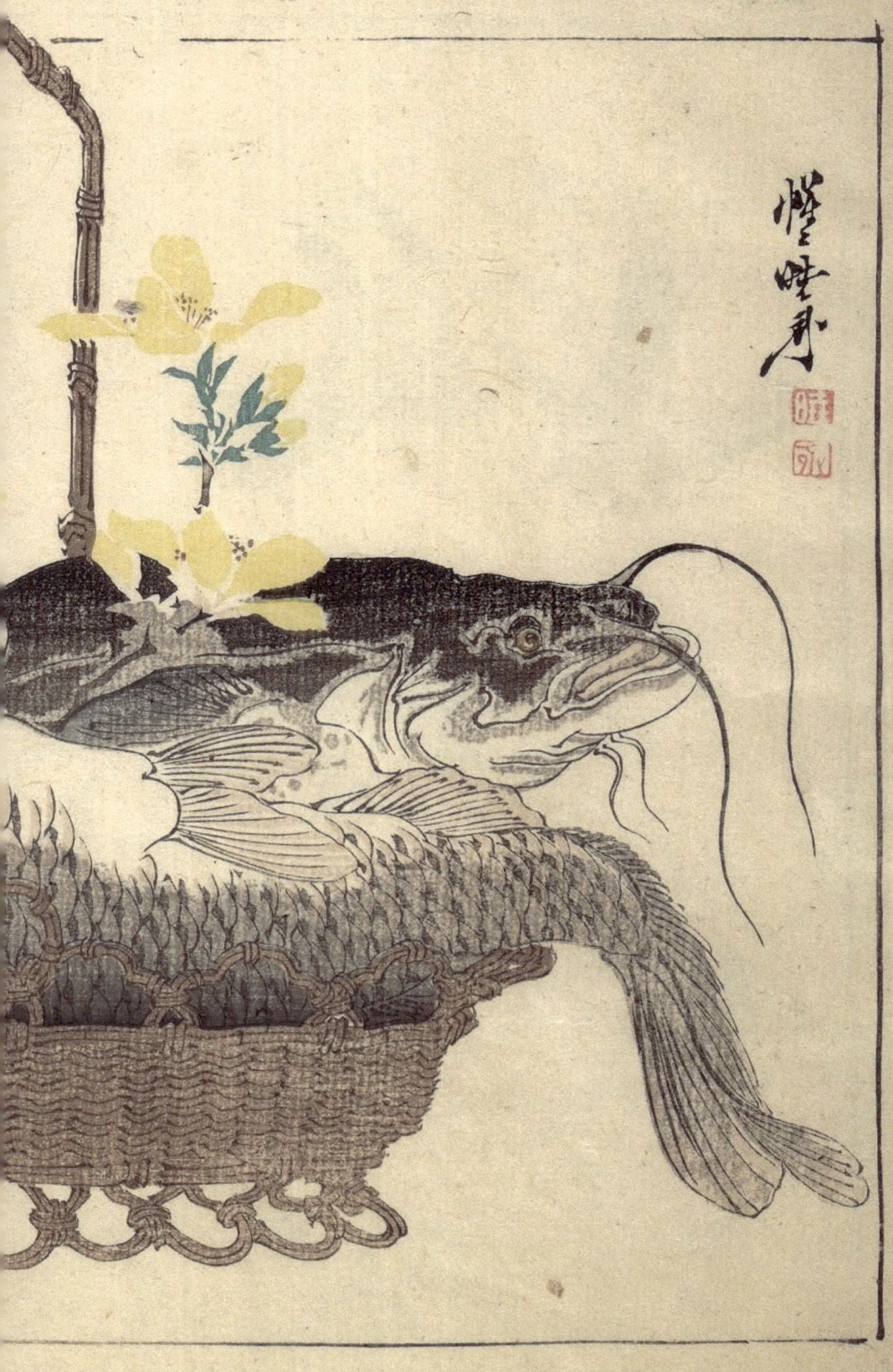

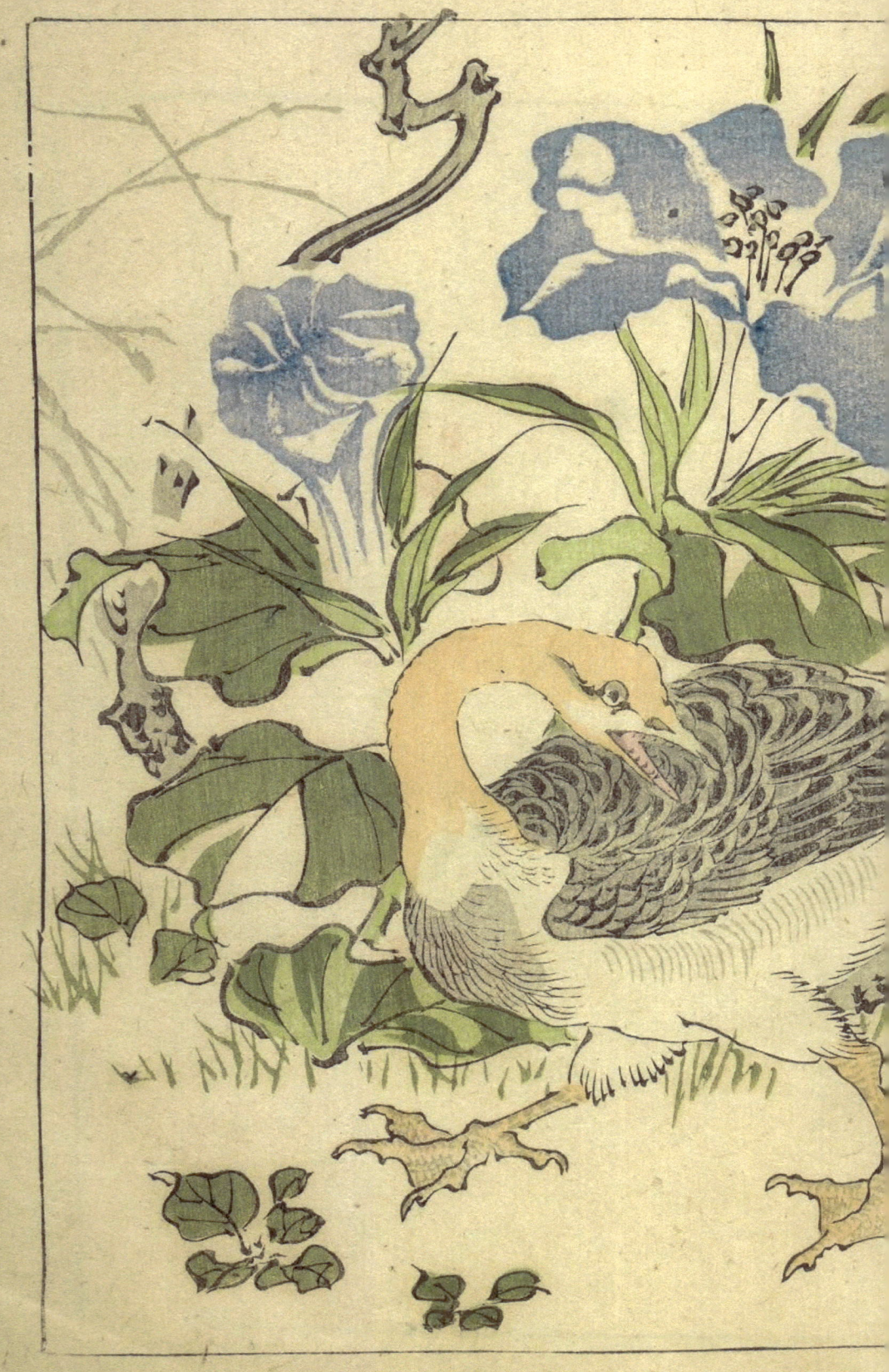

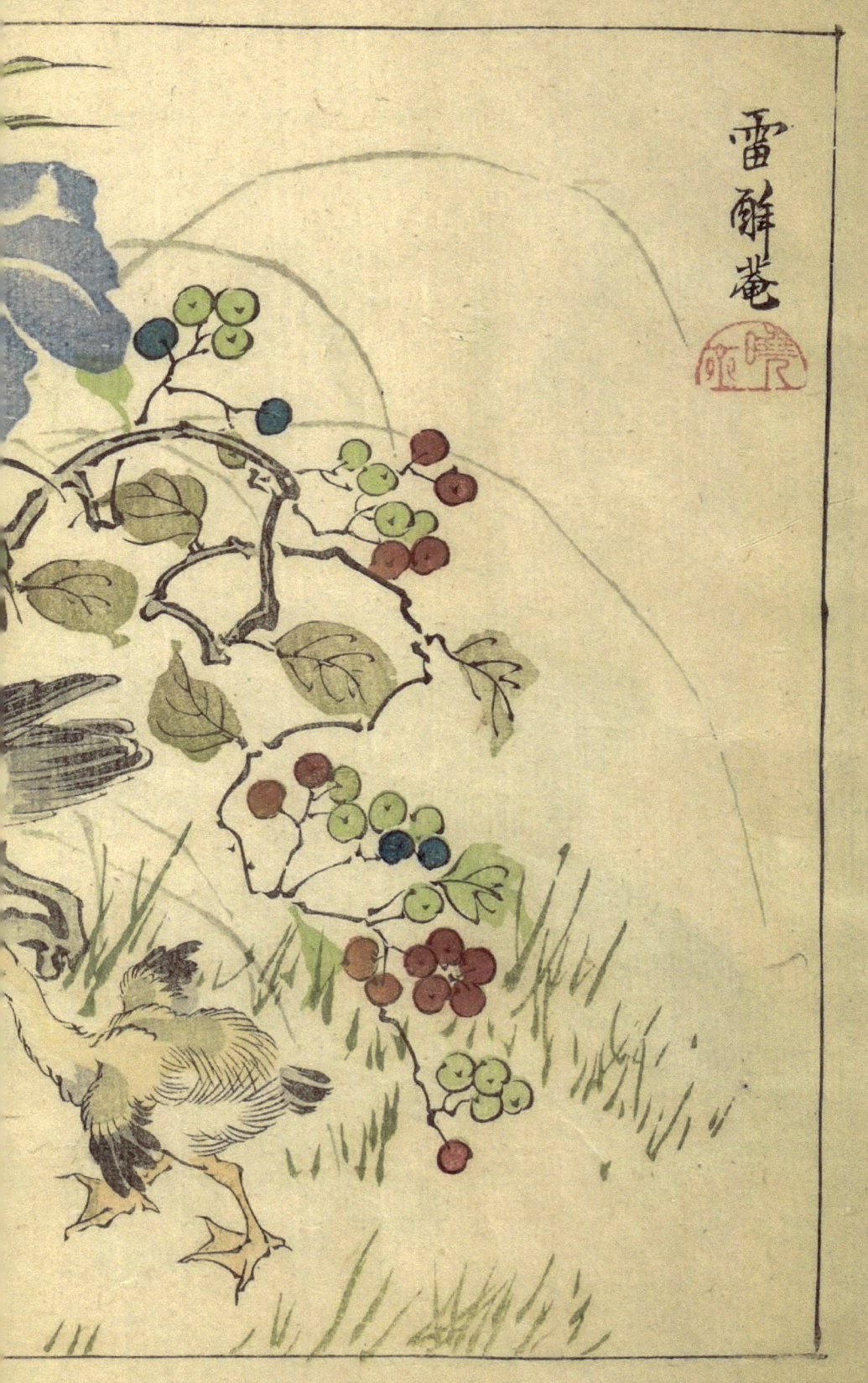

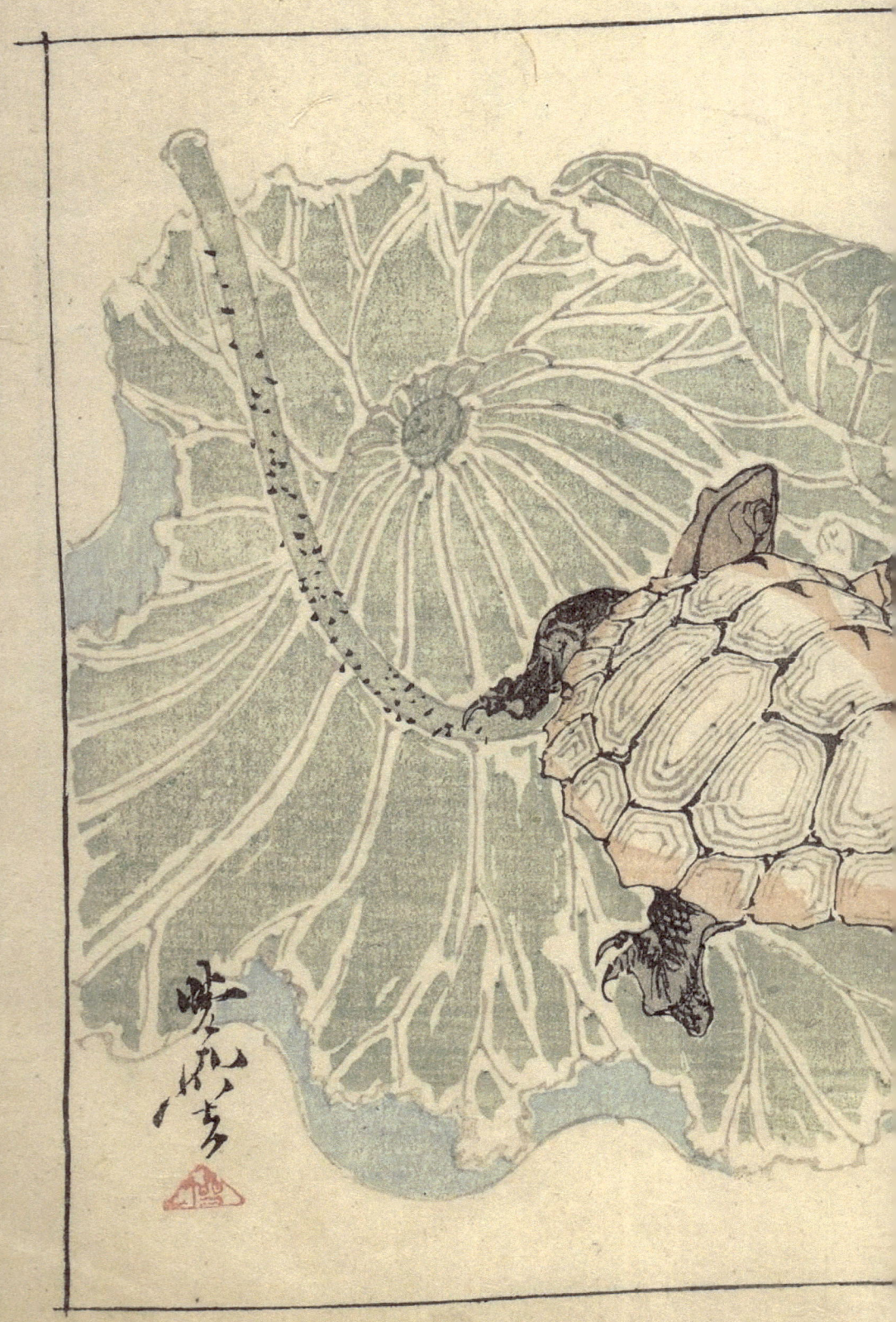

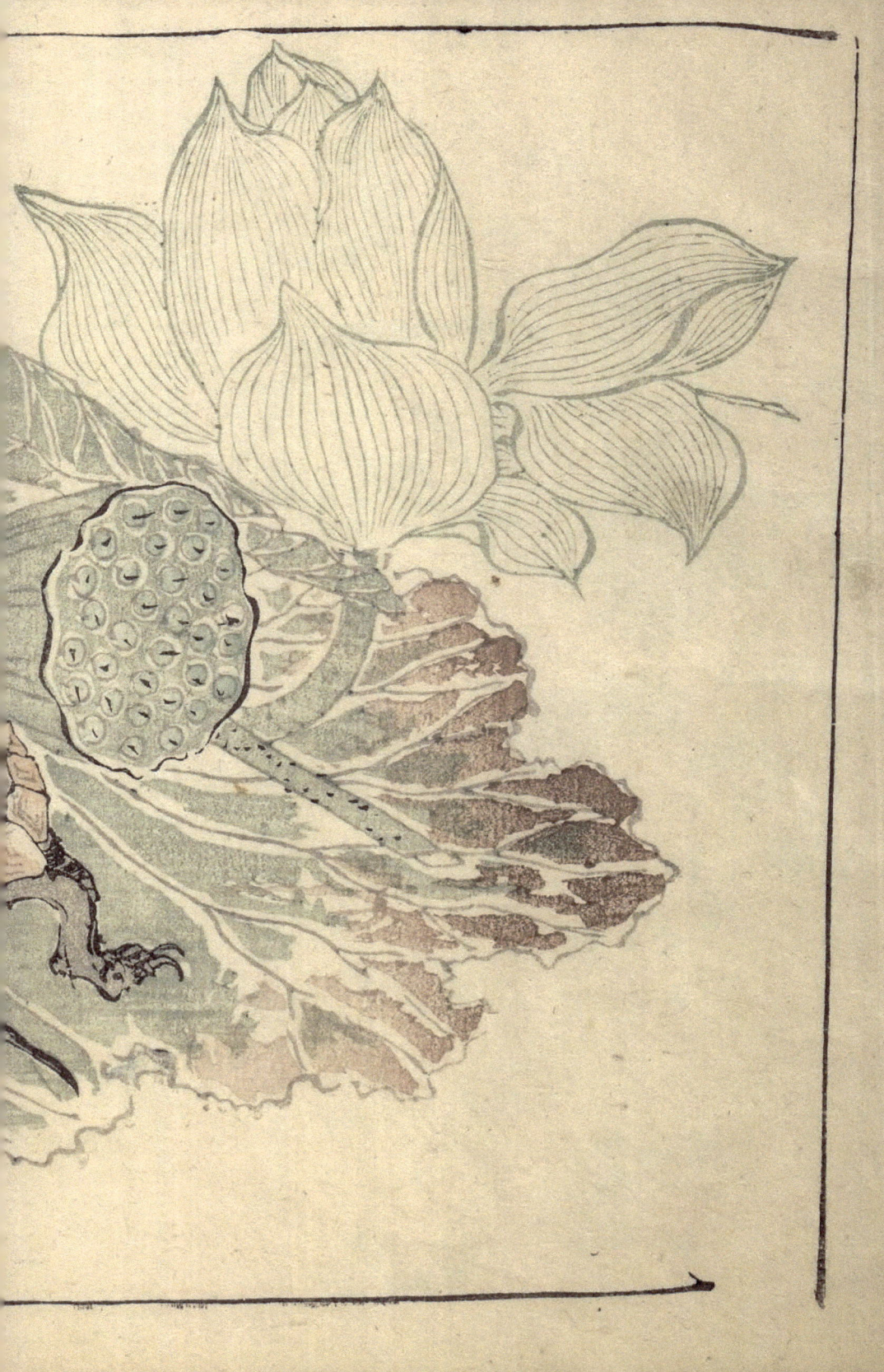

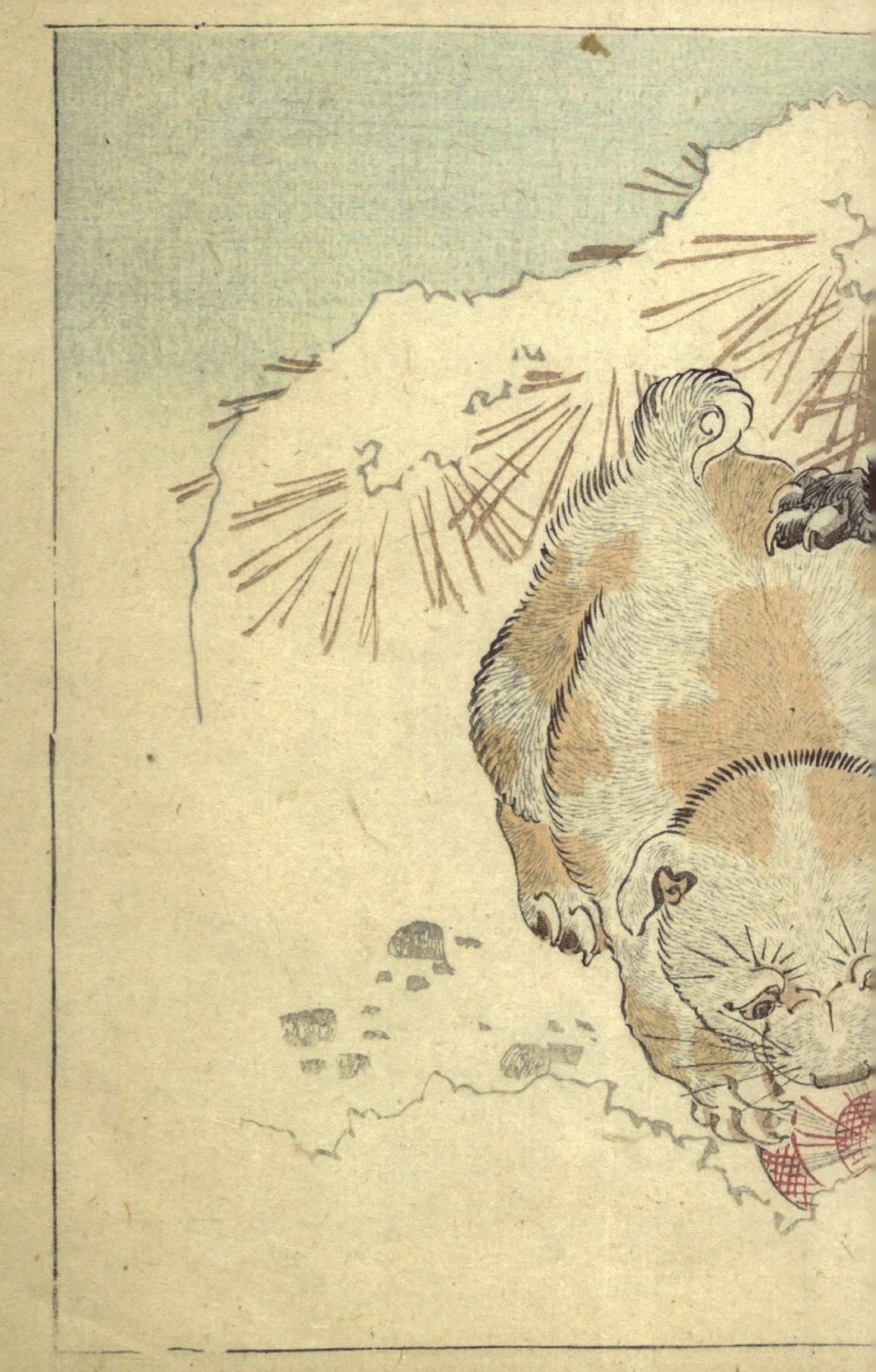

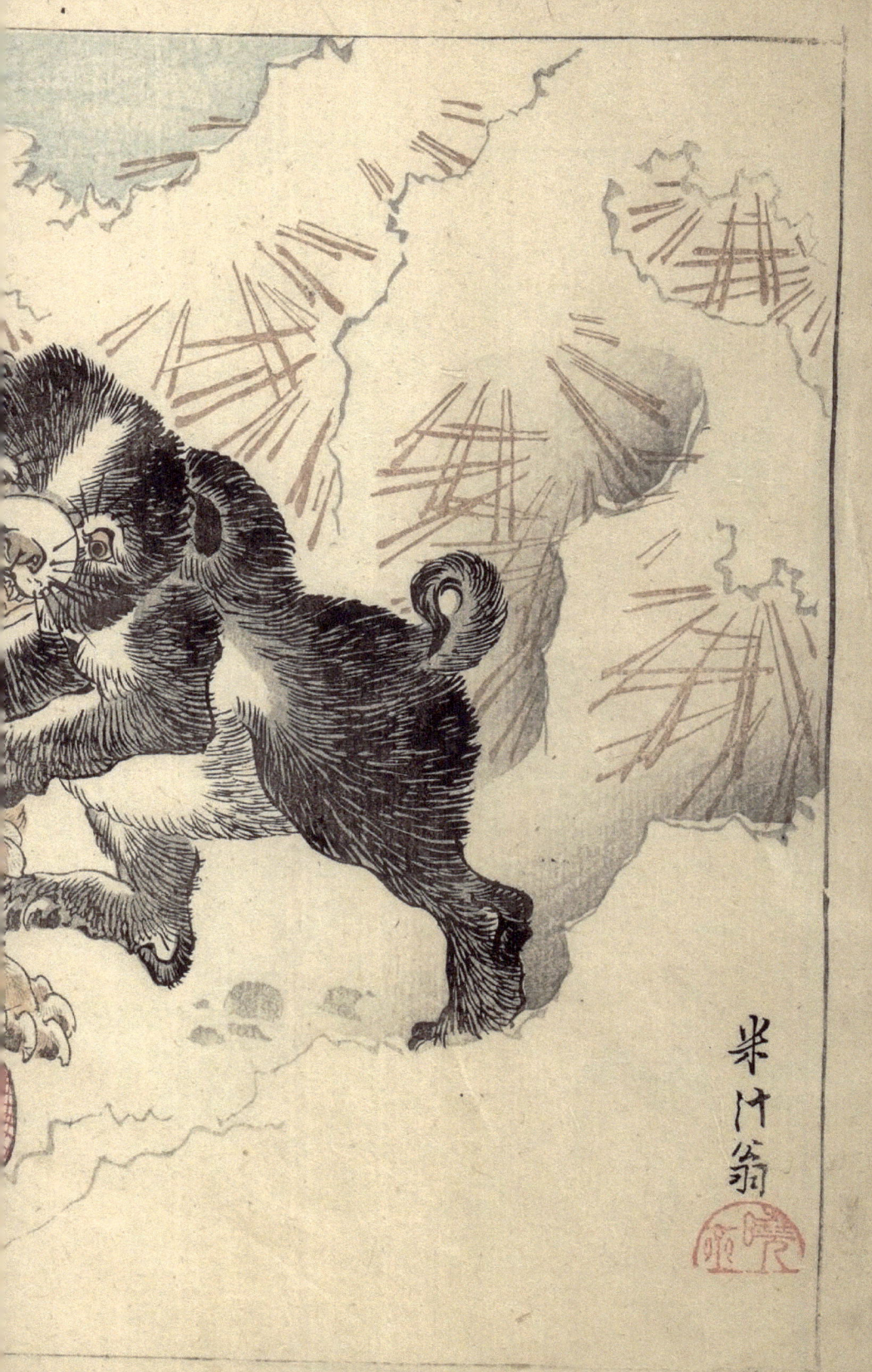

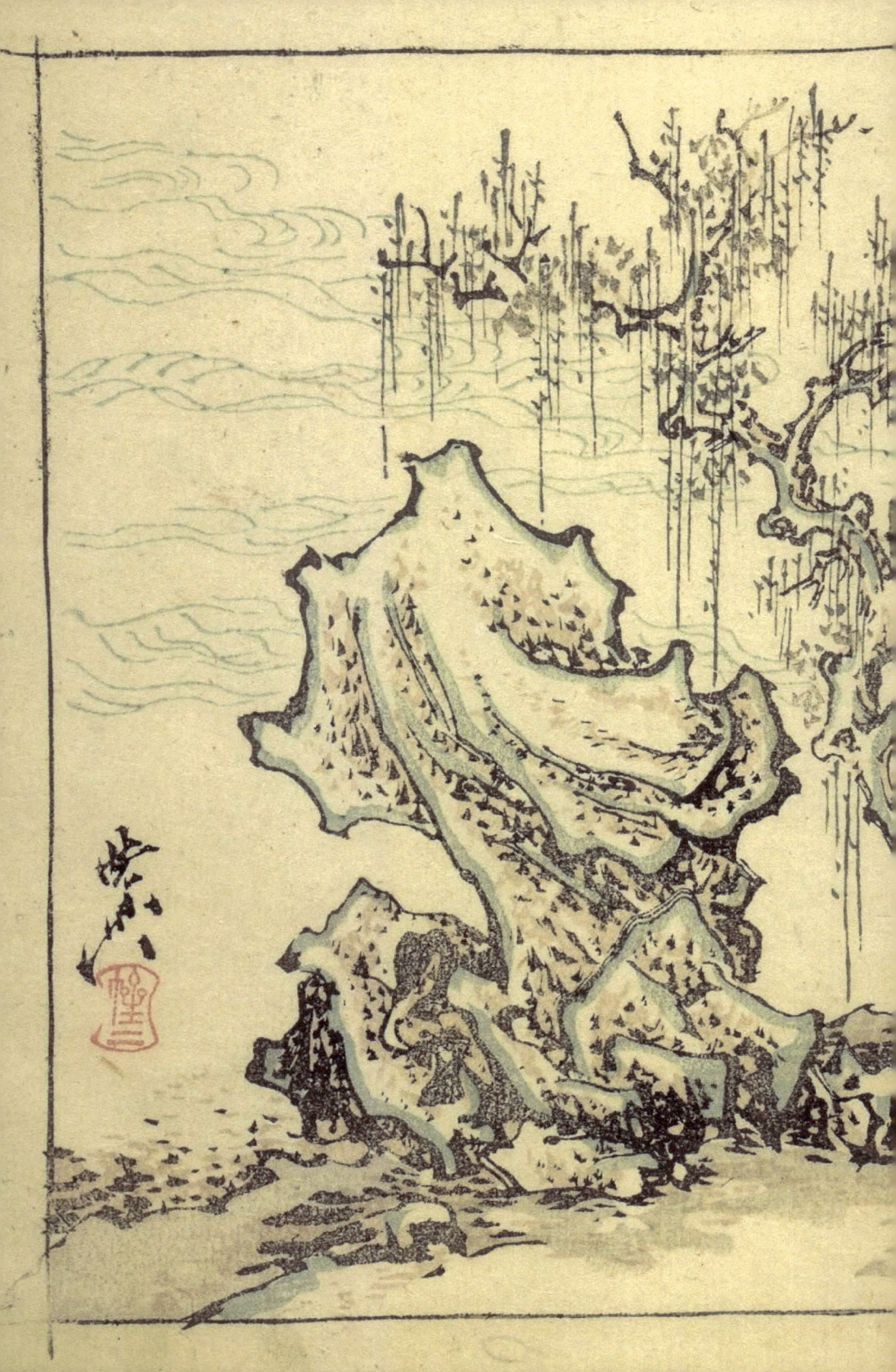

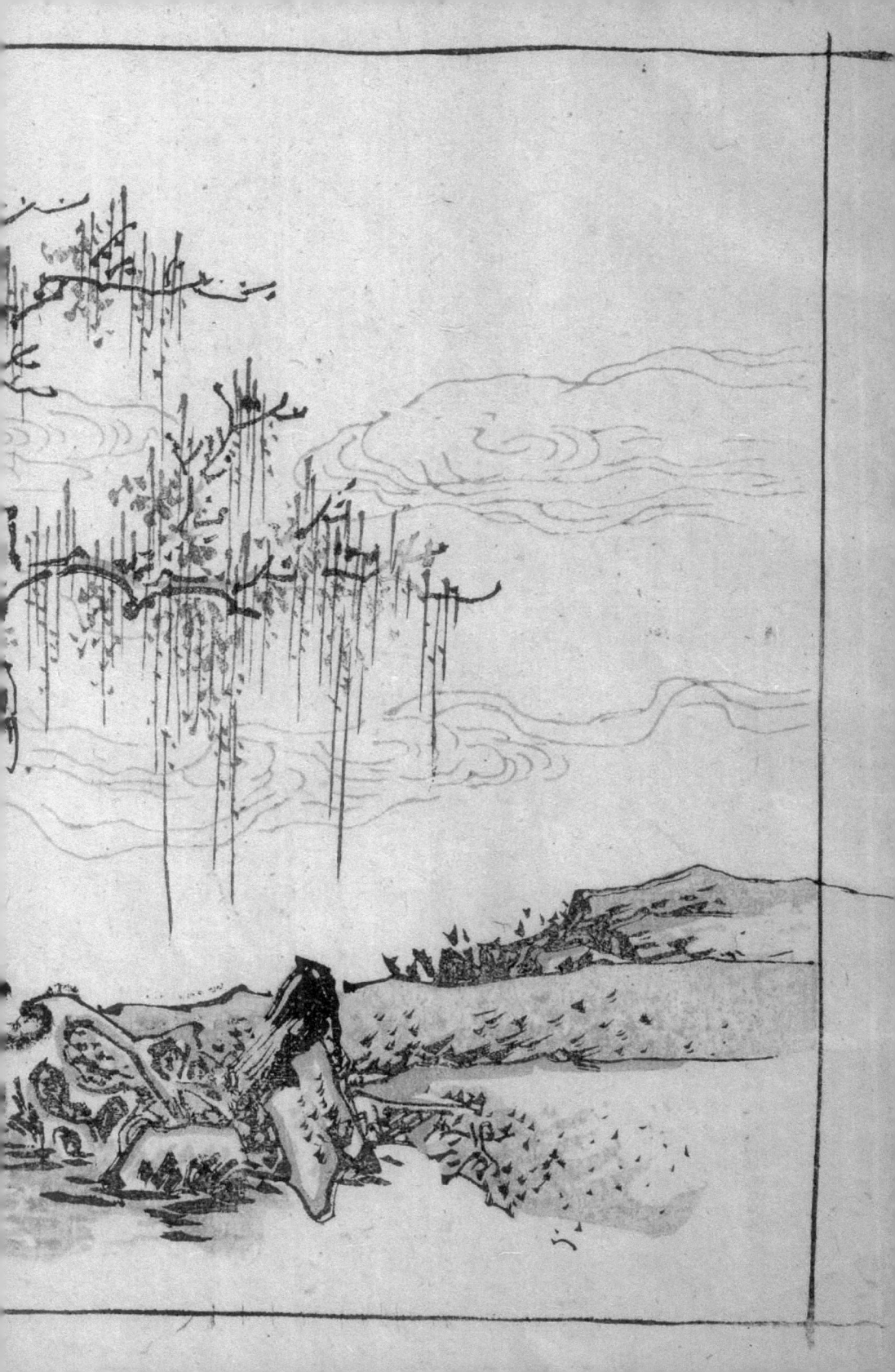

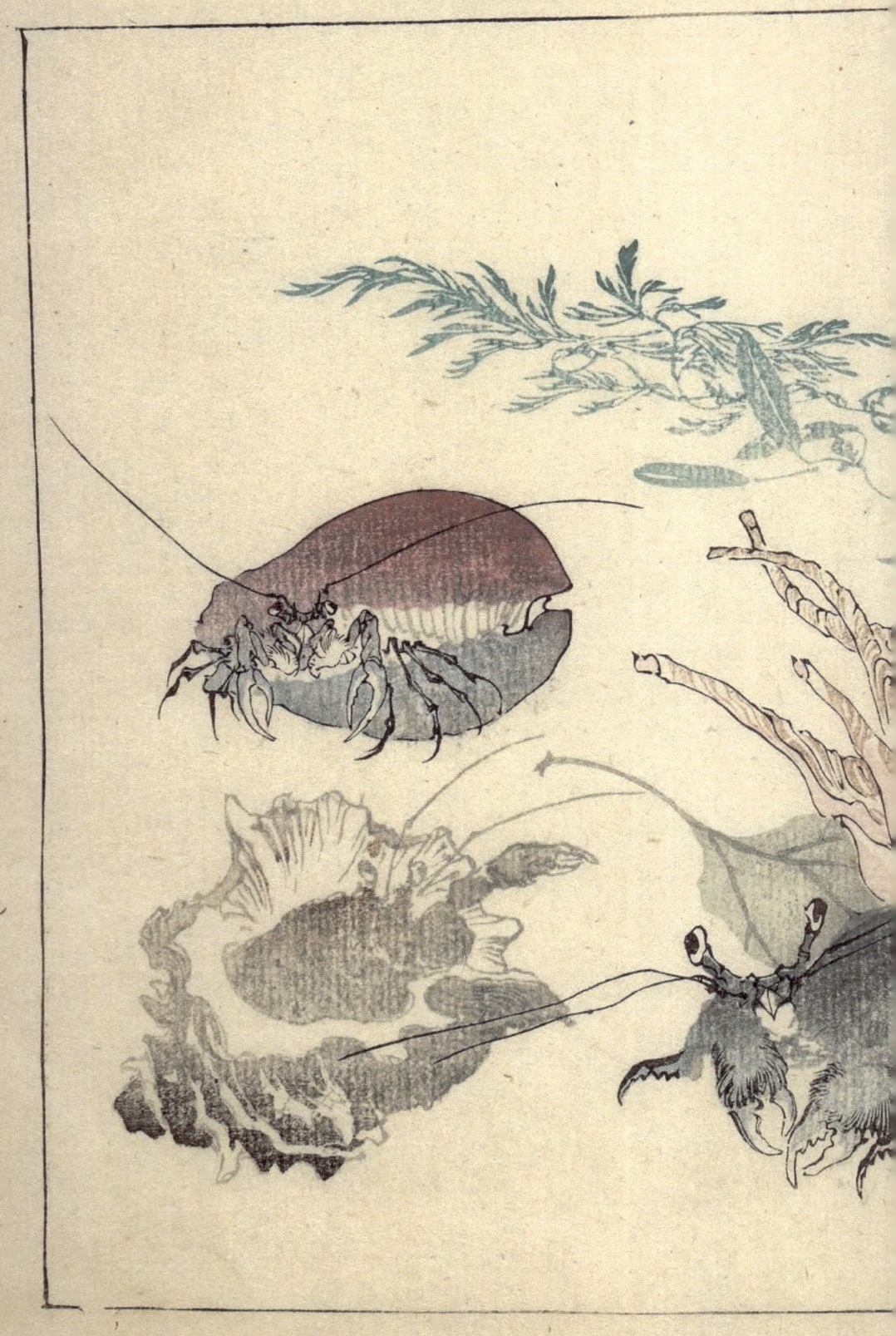

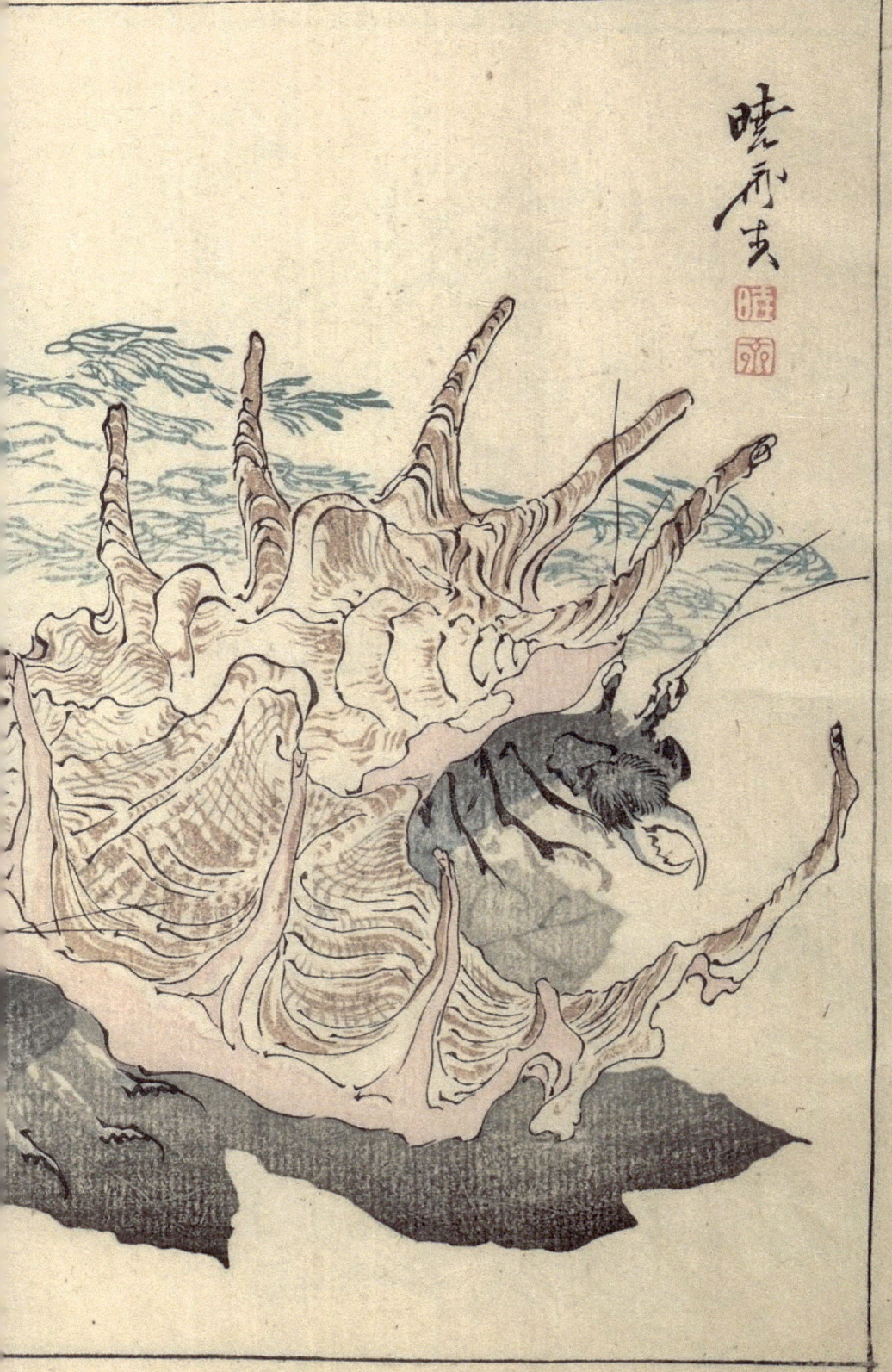

www.ingramcontent.com/pod-product-compliance
Lightning Source LLC
Chambersburg PA
CBHW040338220526
45473CB00009B/2723